TEACHER'S GUIDE

Let Freedom Ring

A HISTORY OF THE JEWS IN THE UNITED STATES

By Jessica B. Weber

BEHRMAN HOUSE, INC.

Dedication

To Jack Weber, a founder of New York Electrical Union Local 3, and his loving wife Lee.

J.W.

C · O · N · T · E · N · T · S

Introduction

HOW TO USE THIS GUIDE

America's Jews have always been few in number, yet they managed to do great and marvelous things. You will be sharing and enriching this dramatic story, the story of how the Jewish people came from nearly every part of the globe in search of freedom and opportunity. You will be teaching your students how they became actors and writers, scientists and doctors, manufacturers and entrepreneurs, and in the process helped shape the history of our country. In sharing with your students our pride in the achievements and the Jewish values our ancestors demonstrate, you will be motivating your students to achieve a new greatness that all Americans can share.

Let Freedom Ring and this Teacher's Guide are divided into twelve chapters. The number of class sessions you devote to each chapter is dependent upon whether you plan to complete the textbook in one semester or whether you have a full year to cover the material. Count the number of class sessions available and divide the material accordingly.

We encourage you to plan your lessons in five-minute to ten-minute segments. A segment of discussion can be followed by an activity in the text; a segment of reading can be followed by a mini-lesson on an individual line in the text; a segment of classroom dramatics can be followed by an examination of a primary source document. This constant alternation makes for a lively classroom atmosphere and typically heightens student interest and response.

Chapter Overview

Each chapter in this guide begins with a brief synopsis of the material presented in the chapter. This is followed by lists of events, places, dates, and terms your students will encounter in the chapter.

Introducing the Lesson

This section provides suggestions for introducing the subject matter to students. In general this section utilizes methods of set induction. Remember, these are only suggestions, and you may, of course, choose to develop lesson plans along different lines based on the same material.

Teaching Opportunities in the Text

This section clarifies and comments on individual lines of the text and suggests ways of building them into mini-lessons.

The Time Line

A time line appears on the first page of each chapter in the textbook. Consider creating and displaying an ongoing time line in your classroom. Students can post the important events and years from each successive chapter on the time line as they proceed through the book.

Jewish Value to Explore

A Jewish value is highlighted and defined in each chapter of this guide for inclusion in your lesson plan.

Suggested Activities

This section suggests a variety of additional activities to consider for your lesson plans. Select the activities that are most appropriate for your students and the time available.

Discussion Questions

Several questions are presented in this section. These can be used at appropriate times in the lesson to check comprehension or to serve as a springboard for class discussion.

Further Research Possibilities

This section suggests enrichment opportunities through further student research.

Primary Source Material

Each chapter in this guide provides source material from the historic period under study. The examination of historic documents, such as letters, newspaper articles, and personal accounts, will help to bring history to life for your students. These materials are prepared as black-line masters and may be photocopied in the quantity you require.

The First Jews in America

Let Freedom Ring (pages 9-14)

Chapter Overview

The Expulsion from Spain in 1492 brought some Jews across the sea to the New World. Several of the men who sailed with Columbus were *conversos*, Jews who had been forcibly converted to the Catholic faith. Among them were his map maker, navigator, interpreter, and surgeon.

Later, other *conversos* settled in Brazil, managing farms and producing sugar. Some even became wealthy. But when the Portuguese took over Brazil, they were forced to flee again.

Some went north to the new colony of New Amsterdam, where the governor, Peter Stuyvesant, tried to expel them. The small band of Jews was finally granted permission to stay by the Dutch West India Company, who ran the colony. Dutch Jews were among the directors of the company. Slowly the Jews in New Amsterdam gained the rights to own land, serve in the local guard, and engage in free trade. By the time of the American Revolution there were fewer than 3,000 Jews in the colonies, still struggling for equal rights.

Important Events Your Students Will Witness:

- **The arrival of the first Jews in the New World:** Luis de Torres, Columbus' interpreter, accompanied the explorer on his famous voyage to the New World and remained there when the ships returned to Spain.
- **The establishment of the first Jewish settlement:** Spanish and Portuguese Jewish *conversos* settled in Recife, Brazil, in the 1500s and remained there until the Portuguese conquered the city in 1654.
- **The beginning of the first Jewish community in North America:** Twenty-three Jews arrived in New Amsterdam and finally became citizens of the colony.

Places Your Students Will Visit

- **Spain:** During the years of the Inquisition and Expulsion.
- **Recife, Brazil:** The first Jewish settlement in America.
- **New Amsterdam:** The Dutch colony that was the site of the first Jewish community in North America.

People Your Students Will Meet Along the Way

- **Luis de Torres:** The first Jew to settle in the New World.
- **Luis de Santangel:** Chancellor of the royal house of Aragon, a *converso* who helped finance Columbus' voyage.

- **Isaac Aboab da Fonseca:** The first rabbi in the New World.
- **Asser Levy:** A successful businessman known for his generosity. He was the first Jew to own property in the colonies.

Important Dates
- **1492:** The first Jews arrived in the New World.
- **1654:** The first Jewish settlement was formed in New Amsterdam.

Terms Your Students Will Be Able to Define
- **Inquisition:** The tribunal of the Catholic Church set up to discover and punish heretics.
- **Converso:** The name given to Jews who converted to the Catholic faith.
- **Crypto Jews (Marranos):** Converts who secretly practiced Judaism.

Introducing the Lesson

Ask the class what they think of when they hear the date 1492. They will probably tell you that it is the year in which Columbus discovered America. Explain that it is also a very important year in Jewish history, because in that year the Jews of Spain were expelled and forced to find new homes in foreign lands. This expulsion is what brought the first Jews to the New World.

Explain that when we learn American history in public school, we are taught the facts that are important to all Americans, but that now we are going to look at the same events with "Jewish eyes." Many people know that Columbus discovered America in 1492, but few people know of the expulsion from Spain that changed Jewish lives forever.

How did Jews help win the American Revolution? Who were the Jews who fought against slavery during the Civil War? How did Jews help settle the West and build a nation of freedom and justice for all? In every age, Jews, using Torah values and moral perspective, intelligence and ingenuity, helped to make this country great. Historical events can be viewed from many angles and perspectives, and our new text will reveal the Jewish angle on the shaping of America. It is our hope that when we are through, you will see a place for yourself in the shaping of our nation, meeting the challenges of the future, not just as an American, but as a Jew.

Teaching Opportunities in the Text

Page 10 How the Jews Helped Columbus
The Jews on Columbus' ships were the map maker, the surgeon, the interpreter, and the navigator. The instruments used by navigators on the seas were also invented by Jews. Why do you think these tasks were likely to be done by Jews?

Page 10 The First Jews in the New World
Speculate for a minute about the life of Luis de Torres. Why do you think he chose to stay in the New World? What might some of his other choices have been?

Page 10 **If you were to write a letter to Jews in Spain today telling them why you think America is a good place to live now, what would you say?**
The letter can be assigned as homework or discussed as a group, with you listing positive points on the chalkboard. If you wish to extend the experience, also list ways in which conditions in America can be improved to make it an even better place to live.

Page 11 **Northward**
As rulers change, life changes for those who live under their rule. The change in Recife from Dutch to Portuguese rule brought great changes for the Jews. What were some of the changes? What were the choices the Jews were presented with at this time? What are some modern examples of a change in government causing a drastic change in the lives of certain ethnic groups?

Page 11 **...but the letters took longer to get to Holland than the Jews took to get to New Amsterdam.**
Imagine writing a letter that took several months to arrive. What does this tell you about the pace of life in the 1500s. What has happened to the pace of our communications today? What new technologies have brought these changes about?

Page 12 **So it happened that after six months at sea, twenty-three penniless Jews came ashore in New Amsterdam...**
Ask your students to put themselves in the place of one of these twenty-three Jewish immigrants and explain how they got there and how they feel about their situation.

Page 12 **It is a wonder of our history that in times of trouble there are often Jews in another part of the world who are ready and able to help. Can you describe recent examples of this?**
Encourage students to consider the rescue of Ethiopian Jewry (Operation Moses) and the ongoing work on behalf of Jews in the former Soviet Union (Operation Exodus). Find out how organizations in your community help Russian emigres to the United States. Is there a way for your students to participate in this work?

Page 14 **...to serve in local guard units...**
You might like to share this additional information with your students:
Asser Levy is remembered for his legal contest with Governor Stuyvesant over the civil rights of the Jews of New Amsterdam. Stuyvesant exempted the Jews from guard duty. Instead he imposed a special monthly tax on them. Levy refused to pay the tax, demanding the right to do civic duty. Despite Stuyvesant's persistent refusal, Levy eventually won his case. As a result, the Jews of New Amsterdam were finally granted full citizenship rights.

The Time Line
The class might begin a time line, posting the important events and years from the chapter. The time line can be lengthened with each successive chapter.

Jewish Value to Explore

▶ **Pidyon sh'vuyim: The mitzvah of rescuing the captive.** As long as Jews have lived among a hostile majority, the mitzvah of "redeeming the captive" (pidyon sh'vuyim) has remained a crucial obligation of a Jewish community.

Suggested Activities

1. A Jew in Spain had to make a choice in 1492. One could become a *converso* and renounce Judaism, or become a *crypto Jew* and be a public Catholic and a secret Jew. Jews could flee to the New World or other countries of Europe or North Africa. Have students make their own choice and write a brief essay to defend their choice.

2. Tell the story of the voyage of Columbus from the perspective of one of the *conversos* on the ship.

3. Imagine your students are all members of the Jewish colony in Brazil. It is 1654 and the Portuguese have just conquered the city. Have the students list the alternatives they have in deciding their future. At the conclusion of the discussion have each make a personal choice as to what he or she would have done. See if the result matches what happened in real life.

4. Learn more about the life of Asser Levy. Discuss the Jewish values that shaped his actions.

5. The Jews of 1492 had to make quick and radical changes in their lives. Compare life in Spain with life in the New World. Have the students list some of the major changes that took place in the lives of those Jews. Then have each student use that list to write a page in the diary of a Spanish boy or girl who traveled from Spain to Brazil and then to New Amsterdam.

Discussion Questions

1. What was the Spanish Inquisition? How did it affect the Jews of Spain and Portugal?

2. What two important events occurred in 1492?

3. What important tasks did the *conversos* on Columbus' ships perform?

4. Why did Luis de Torres decide to stay in the New World?

5. What was the major difference between the astrolabe and "Jacob's Staff," two navigational instruments invented by Jews?

6. Where was the first Jewish settlement in the New World? How did the Jews who lived there make a living?

7. Describe the difficulties the Jews had when they reached the colony of New Amsterdam? Why did they experience these difficulties? How were they resolved?

8. What were some of the rights the Jews had to fight for in the New World from the very beginning?

Further Research Possibilities

Research the important role that Jews played as map makers and navigators in Europe during the fifteenth and sixteenth centuries. How did their work change history?

Primary Source Worksheet

Photocopy the black line master on the next page in the quantity you require and distribute a copy to each student. After your students have read the letters, pose these questions:

1. If you had been in a position to decide the fate of the small community of destitute Jews that landed in New Amsterdam, what would your decision have been? Why?

2. What was the actual final decision?

3. How do you think Governor Stuyvesant reacted to the decision? Was he bound by it?

4. Although America was founded by various peoples searching for religious freedom, they did not necessarily wish to grant full freedom to everyone in their new colonies. How does this historic episode suggest the continuous battle for religious freedom that Jews would have to fight in this new land?

PRIMARY SOURCE MATERIAL

▶ You have read that Governor Peter Stuyvesant wrote to his employers, the directors of the Dutch West India Company, asking for permission to force the Jews to leave New Amsterdam. That letter was written on September 22, 1654, and here is a part of it.

The Jews who have arrived would nearly all like to remain here, but learning that they (with their customary usury and deceitful trading with the Christians) were very repugnant to the people having the most affection for you; also fearing that owing to their present indigence they might become a charge in the coming winter, we have, for the benefit of this weak and newly developing place deemed it useful to require them to depart; praying of your worships that the deceitful race be not allowed further to infect and trouble this new colony... .

▶ Meanwhile Jews in Holland petitioned the company on behalf of the Jews in New Amsterdam. Their persuasive arguments affected the final decision. Here are parts of the petition.

Your Honors raise obstacles to the giving of permits or passports to the Portuguese Jews to travel and to go to reside in New Netherland, which if persisted in will result to the great disadvantage of the Jewish nation. It also can be of no advantage to the general Company but rather damaging.

It is well known to your Honors that the Jewish nation in Brazil have at all times been faithful and have striven to guard and maintain that place, risking for that purpose their possessions and their blood.

Yonder land is extensive and spacious. The more of loyal people that go to live there, the better it is in regard to the population of the country as in regard to the payment of various excises and taxes which may be imposed there, and in regard to the increase of trade, and also to the importation of all the necessaries that may be sent there.

Your Honors should also please consider that many of the Jewish nation are principal shareholders in the Company. They having always striven their best for the Company, and many of their nation have lost immense and great capital in its shares and obligations... .

2 A New World with Old Values

Let Freedom Ring (pages 15-20)

Chapter Overview

Jews who chose to make the New World their home in the 1600s found that they could live peacefully and in accordance with Jewish tradition because the values of daily life in the early colonies were taken from the Bible. They enjoyed relative freedom and safety in this environment. As communities developed, synagogues were built and became the focal point for the activities of the community. Many Jews played important roles in the Revolutionary War as well as in the life of the early colonies.

Important Events Your Students Will Witness

- **The founding of Rhode Island in 1636:** Roger Williams founded the colony so that all people could have a place to worship in freedom. Jews were attracted to this idea, and many chose to settle in Rhode Island.

- **The American Revolution:** Some 100 Jews fought in the Continental Army with George Washington, although some Jews remained loyal to the British government.

Places Your Students Will Visit

- **Newport, Rhode Island:** The site of the Touro Synagogue, the oldest synagogue building in the United States today.

- **The seaports of New York, Newport, Philadelphia, and Charleston:** Where Jews settled and became important merchants and shipowners.

People Your Students Will Meet Along the Way

- **Roger Williams:** Founder of the colony of Rhode Island.

- **George Washington:** Hero of the Revolution and later president of the United States. He was a champion of the cause of liberty and justice for all.

- **Haym Salomon:** Money broker who gave much of his fortune to support the Revolutionary War and the new government of the United States.

- **Aaron Lopez:** An observant Jew whose home and warehouse were confiscated by the British because of his support of the patriots.

- **Rebecca Gratz:** A tireless worker and fund-raiser for the Orphan Society, the Hebrew Sunday School Society, and other communal associations she founded in Philadelphia.

- **Gershom Mendes Seixas:** The first American-born religious leader of a Jewish congregation.

Important Dates

- **1636:** The colony of Rhode Island was founded.
- **1728:** Construction on the first synagogue in America was begun.
- **1775:** The thirteen colonies revolted against the British.

Terms Your Students Will Be Able to Define

- **Sephardim:** Jews from southern Europe, North Africa, and Asia.
- **Ashkenazim:** Jews from northern Europe, England, and Germany.
- **Broker:** A person whose job it is to sell merchandise for cash.

Introducing the Lesson

Ask your students to imagine that they are a part of a small group of Jews moving to the New World. They wish to begin a new life as a functioning Jewish community. What essential items would they need immediately? Are there items they would need to bring with them? What are some of the institutions they need to plan and form? Would the prospect of this adventure seem exciting or difficult? Would they need leadership? List the items that the students suggest on the chalkboard by category and relate them to the Jewish experience in the early colonies (Pages 15 and 16 of the text).

Teaching Opportunities in the Text

Page 15 **The Thanksgiving holiday in America was patterned after the Jewish festival of Sukkot.**
Sukkot is known in the Bible as "Tabernacles" or "feast of ingathering." It celebrates the gathering in from the threshing floor and winepress at the change of the season. Ask your students to compare and contrast the celebrations of Sukkot and Thanksgiving for similarities and differences.

Page 15 **The colonies were ruled by laws taken from the Christian Old Testament...**
Not only did the founders of our nation look to the Bible for their values and way of life, they were also interested in the Hebrew language. Harvard University offered Hebrew as a course in the early 1700s, calling it "instruction in the primitive tongue in order to gain better acquaintance with the sacred Oracles of the Old Testament." Judah Monis published a Hebrew Grammar with Harvard in 1735. He had converted to Christianity in 1722 and received an appointment as instructor in Hebrew at Harvard. Why did the colonists think that the Hebrew language was important?

Page 16 **The synagogue cared for the Jewish cemetery...**
When new Jewish communities formed, one of the first things they always established was a Jewish cemetery. Why do you think this was such a priority?

Page 18 **Some 100 Jews fought in the Continental Army under George Washington.**

Some Jews sided with the British during the Revolution, and others sided with George Washington and the Continental Army. Have your students discuss what might motivate a new immigrant to choose one side or the other.

Page 20 **...freedom of religion became the national policy of the United States.**

Freedom of religion is a wonderful thing. After years of persecution, Jews felt "many marvelous deliverances that we have experienced since the time of our redemption from Egypt." These are the words of Gershom Mendes Seixas in 1798. What did Seixas mean by this? What are some of the implications of religious freedom? Freedom offers both the right to worship and the right not to worship. How has this freedom affected the American Jewish community?

Jewish Value to Explore

▶ **Tzedakah:** The mitzvah of offering help to the needy. The act of "doing the right thing." The newly formed congregations of the New World took care of the sick, the aged, and the poor. They began organizations for orphaned children, education, etc., always stressing that the needy receive these services for free.

▶ **Kehilah:** The concept of community. Wherever Jews gathered, they formed communities to support each other, to provide education, kosher food, opportunity for prayer, proper burial, etc. Community is an important aspect of Jewish life, both in the past and today.

Suggested Activities

1. Form two teams for a debate on the question: "I am a Jew living in the New World. The Revolution is about to begin. Should I support the British or the Continental Army of George Washington?"

2. Pretend that you are Gershom Mendes Seixas and are speaking on Rosh Hashanah in your synagogue in the New World. What type of sermon would you give? What issues would be important to you? Deliver your sermon to the class.

3. Pretend that you are Rebecca Gratz and you need to raise money for one of your charities. What would you say? Deliver a fund-raising speech to the class.

Discussion Questions

1. What are some of the Torah laws that early American Christians incorporated into their lives in the New World?

2. Why were Jews known as "People of the Book?"

3. What were some of the community functions that took place in the early

synagogues of America?

4. Why was the colony of Rhode Island founded?

5. Why was it logical for Jews to be involved in shipping and international trade?

Further Research Possibilities

Learn more about the community you live in. When did the first Jews come to your town? Where did they come from? When did they build their first synagogue and incorporate the first cemetery? Are these places still in existence? Were there any well-known personalities that left their mark in some way?

Primary Source Worksheet

Photocopy the black line master on the next page in the quantity you require and distribute a copy to each student. After your students have read the letter, pose these questions:

1. What characteristics must the schoolmaster have to be employed by Shearith Israel?

2. What things does this letter tell you about what school was like in those days?

3. What are some of the things that made it different from the school you attend today?

4. Pretend you are a candidate for the job of schoolmaster. Write a brief letter describing yourself to the congregation.

PRIMARY SOURCE MATERIAL

This letter was written in 1760 by a member of Congregation Shearith Israel in New York. It contains instructions for hiring a schoolmaster for the children of the congregation.

New York, December 16, 1760

Sir:

You will be good enough to engage a suitable master capable to teach our children the Hebrew language. English and Spanish he ought to know, but he will not suit unless he understands Hebrew and English at least. A single modest sober person would be most agreeable. He must oblige himself to keep a publick school at the usual hours of the forenoons on every customary day at our yeshiba. Children whose parents are in needy circumstances he must teach gratis. His salary shall be first at forty pounds, New York money per year, and shall commence from the day of his arrival here ...

Religion, Slavery, and War

Let Freedom Ring (pages 21-27)

Chapter Overview

From 1840 to 1869 the Jewish population of the United States increased dramatically because of a large influx of Jews from Germany. They settled in the cities of the West and established new communities. Both the Reform and Conservative movements were born in this new environment of freedom and change. As the Civil War gripped America, Jews fought in both the Union and Confederate armies, dividing their political loyalties. They remained united, however, when it came to such issues as providing matzah for the war-torn southern Jews on the eve of Passover.

Important Events Your Students Will Witness

- **Large-scale immigration to the United States:** From 1840 to 1869 the Jewish population of the United States rose from 15,000 to 150,000. Many of these immigrants were German. They moved west into the cities of the frontier.
- **The founding of Hebrew Union College, the Union of American Hebrew Congregations:** Rabbi Isaac Mayer Wise worked to build a unique "reform" Judaism to Jewish life in America.
- **The Civil War:** Jews served in both the Union and Confederate armies during the Civil War.

Places Your Students Will Visit

- **Cities such as Pittsburgh, New Orleans, and St. Louis:** Many German immigrants moved westward, building synagogues for their growing communities.
- **Cincinnati, Ohio:** The home of the first rabbinic college in the United States, founded by Isaac Mayer Wise in 1875.

People Your Students Will Meet Along the Way

- **Isaac Mayer Wise:** German-immigrant rabbi who worked to reform Judaism to fit life in America.
- **Isaac Leeser:** A traditional Jew from Philadelphia who translated the Hebrew Bible into English and made English sermons a regular part of his Sabbath morning service.
- **Judah P. Benjamin:** A successful Louisiana lawyer who became a U.S. senator and, during the Civil War, secretary of war and secretary of state for the Confederacy.
- **Rabbi Jacob Frankel:** The first Jewish chaplain in the U.S. army. He was appointed by President Lincoln.

19

- **Ernestine Rose:** Woman who spoke out on issues such as slavery and the rights of women.

Important Dates
- **1873:** The Union of American Hebrew Congregations was founded.
- **1875:** Hebrew Union College in Cincinnati was founded.
- **1861:** The Civil War began.

Terms Your Students Will Be Able to Define
- **Chaplain:** A member of the clergy officially attached to the armed forces to serve the religious needs of military personnel.
- **Suffrage:** The right and privilege of voting. The Constitution of the United States originally gave this right only to male property owners.

Introducing the Lesson

Life in America brought some problems to observant Jews. Ask you students to imagine the following:

The year is 1858. You are a new immigrant to the United States and have recently settled in Cincinnati, Ohio. Your rabbi back in Europe warned you that if you came to America you would not be able to continue to keep the Sabbath, but you had promised that you would. Now you have a job in a factory and you are told you must work on Saturday. How would you respond? What other Jewish observances might it be difficult for you to follow?

Teaching Opportunities in the Text

Page 22 **Unlike more traditional Jews, Wise felt it was necessary to change Jewish laws...**

What were some of the laws that Jews found it difficult to observe once they moved into the cities of the western United States? How would you have dealt with these problems? Was Isaac Mayer Wise's solution a good one? Why or why not? How do some of the reforms of Isaac Mayer Wise still affect us today?

Page 23 **Where are rabbis trained today?**

The schools listed in this box are all rabbinic seminaries. What is a rabbinic seminary? What subjects are studied there? How long must one study in order to become a rabbi?

Page 24 **Nearly 7,000 Jews fought for the Union during the Civil War. Another 3,000 served in the Confederate army.**

A Jewish member of the Union army, in a letter he wrote during the war, stated that while there were many Jewish soldiers, they "do not care to make their religion a matter of notoriety as it would at once involve them in an intricate controversial disquisition with the Christian chaplains, for which they do not always feel themselves qualified." What does this statement mean? How would you feel in that situation? Would you feel comfortable telling everyone you were Jewish?

What did he mean by "feel themselves unqualified"? We should note that the same writer also stated that he was aware of no incidents of anti-Semitism among the men and that he felt a pervading air of tolerance in the army.

Page 25 **Rabbi Jacob Frankel was the first Jewish chaplain appointed by Abraham Lincoln.**
What is a military chaplain? What does the job entail? Why did Lincoln add rabbis to the list of military chaplains?

Page 26 **...Ernestine Rose spoke out publicly on issues like slavery and the rights of women.**
The work of Ernestine Rose shows her interest in the Jewish concept of *tikun olam*, or repairing the world. What are some of the ways Ernestine Rose worked toward *tikun olam?*

Page 26 **...General Ulysses S. Grant accused the Jews of using the war to make large profits for themselves.**
General Grant issued orders to expel all Jewish traders from the area under his command. President Lincoln rescinded the order after protests from Jews around the country. Even though this was an anti-Semitic incident, what made it different from incidents that might have occurred back in Europe?

Jewish Value to Explore

▶ **Tzedakah:** The *mitzvah* of offering help to the needy. The act of "doing the right thing." At the close of the Civil War the Jews of New York and Philadelphia sent thousands of pounds of matzah to Savannah so that the Jews of Georgia could celebrate the Passover holiday.

▶ **K'lal Yisrael:** The unity of the Jewish people. The many ways in which Jews in the North helped Jews in the South get back on their feet after the Civil War ended demonstrates the principle of Jews' uniting to care for one another.

▶ **Tikun olam:** The process of repairing the world. Social Reformers like Ernestine Rose made the pursuit of a better world for all people the focus of their life's work.

Suggested Activities

1. Pretend you are a young person from a Jewish family in the North. You run off and enlist in the Union army. State your reasons in a letter that you write home to your parents.

2. You are a German Jew thinking of immigration to America. List the pros and cons of the situation and come to a decision. Share it with the class.

3. Create a collage of pictures that express the issues that were important to Ernestine Rose. Discuss how her life's work has succeeded, and how it progresses today.

Discussion Questions

1. Why did German Jews decide to come to America during the years 1840–1869? Where primarily did they choose to settle?

2. Who was Isaac Mayer Wise? What were some of his major accomplishments?

3. How does the concept of American freedom affect the way we practice Judaism today?

4. What were some of the ritual changes that some Jews chose to make in America? Why did they feel these changes were necessary?

5. Discuss ways in which Jews were involved in the Civil War?

6. Who was Ernestine Rose and what were her major accomplishments?

7. Who was Judah P. Benjamin? What were his major accomplishments?

Further Research Possibilities

1. Are there synagogues or businesses in your community that were founded between 1840 and 1869? Are the original founding families still involved in their operation? Use your research skills to learn more about your Jewish community during this period.

2. Learn more about Judah P. Benjamin. Write a report about his life. Dress up as Judah P. Benjamin and tell the class about yourself.

3. There have been several incidents of anti-Semitism in the government of United States like the one described in the text involving Ulysses S. Grant (page 26). Learn what legal mechanisms are available today in our country to fight incidents of anti-Semitism. What are some of the laws and statutes that protect Jews from such attacks?

4. Research whether your synagogue is a member of a movement, such as The Union of American Hebrew Congregations, United Synagogue of Conservative Judaism, the Jewish Reconstructionist Federation, or other group as described on page 22 of the text. Why do these movements exist? In what ways does your synagogue participate in its movement?

Primary Source Worksheet

Photocopy the black line master on the next page in the quantity you require and distribution a copy to each student. After your students have read the letter, ask them to imagine the following:

The year is 1870. You are a member of the board of directors of Congregation Mikveh Israel in Savannah, Georgia. This week you will be attending a board meeting where the reforms listed above will be discussed and debated.

Formulate your position for or against each one. Do you think your synagogue should reform or maintain the old traditions. Prepare to debate others with opposing views at the board meeting.

▶ The first Reform congregations started out as traditional. Although no two congregations followed the exact same pattern, here is a list of some of the changes that took place between 1848 and 1901.

System of fines and penalties for violation of Sabbath and holidays eliminated.

Prayer for the government read in English.

Men and women permitted to sit together during services.

Mixed choir of men and women introduced.

Elimination of second-day holiday observance.

Introduction of organ music.

Head covering (kippot) made optional.

Confirmation for boys and girls instituted.

Union Prayer Book adopted.

Late Friday evening service instituted.

Jewish Life in the 1800s

Let Freedom Ring (pages 28-35)

Chapter Overview

Many Jews were among the American pioneers who moved west in the 1800s. Often they were German Jewish peddlers who later became merchants and store owners. Some Jews followed the dream of wealth and fortune and traveled west with the "gold rush" across the Rocky Mountains to California.

Jews began to enter all walks of life in America. Uriah Phillips Levy was the first Jewish commodore. Levi Strauss sold the first blue jeans. Many Jews were known as great philanthropists, making large fortunes and sharing them with the poor.

Important Events Your Students Will Witness

- **The Louisiana Purchase:** President Jefferson purchased the Louisiana territory from France in 1803, providing land and economic opportunity for Americans who chose to travel west.

- **The California "Gold Rush":** Gold was discovered in California in 1848, providing incentive for thousands to travel west to seek their fortune.

Places Your Students Will Visit

- **San Francisco, 1849:** Where Yom Kippur services were held for all the Jews who were in California.

- **Miami, Key West, and Jacksonville:** Jews were among the early founders of these Florida cities.

People Your Students Will Meet Along the Way

- **Levi Strauss:** Businessman who followed the gold seekers west and sold a new kind of denim work pants.

- **Josephine Sarah Marcus:** The Jewish common-law wife of lawman Wyatt Earp.

- **Mordecai Manuel Noah:** Man who tried to establish a Jewish colony near Buffalo, New York—but no settlers came.

- **Uriah Phillips Levy:** The first Jewish commodore in the U.S. Navy.

- **The Straus family:** The owners of Macy's department store in New York City. Oscar Straus was the first Jew to serve in a U.S. presidential cabinet. Isidor Straus developed the Educational Alliance of New York. Nathan Straus was known as a great philanthropist.

Important Dates
- **1803:** President Jefferson purchased the Louisiana territory from France.
- **1848:** Gold was discovered in California.

Terms Your Students Will Be Able to Define
- **Peddler:** A person who made a living by traveling to remote frontier settlements selling household goods.
- **Commodore:** A naval officer ranking above a captain and below a rear admiral.

Introducing the Lesson
Read the following to the class:

The year is 1851. Abraham Abrahamson dropped everything to travel by steamer from the east coast of the United States to San Francisco. He had heard stories of those who had become instantly wealthy in the "gold rush," and he wanted to get in on the action too.

He wrote: "Everywhere, one heard of the fame of the newly discovered land of gold and how so many people have quickly and easily become rich there. Everywhere, I saw people, coming from there with large chunks of gold ... and who lived in grand style."

He went on to describe an arduous journey he took by sea and land, and to express excitement at arriving in San Francisco. Once there, he found prices high and conditions difficult as he wrote, "One can imagine the rest when one knows that I had to pay one dollar for an egg."

Ask your students to imagine that they live in the eastern United States and that they are struggling to make a living as a peddler of household goods. They work very hard and earn small amounts of money. One day they hear the stories of gold being discovered in California, just as Abraham Abrahamson did. What would they choose to do? Would they stay and persist or drop everything and go west in pursuit of a dream?

Use the discussion that ensues to introduce the topic of the Jewish pioneers who traveled west to many different cities in pursuit of wealth, peaceful living, and freedom from persecution.

Teaching Opportunities in the Text

Page 28 **Many of these were German Jewish peddlers who later became merchants and store owners.**
What was the life of a peddler like? Why did so many Jewish immigrants choose to be peddlers? Peddlers provided a needed service in remote locations throughout the United States. Why was the service they provided so necessary? Why did peddlers give up their bundles and carts to become merchants and store owners? Do you think you would have enjoyed the life of a peddler? Why or why not?

Page 28 **The Louisiana Purchase**
The purchase of the Louisiana territory more than doubled the size of the United States. What effect did this have on American history and the choices

Americans made in the 1800s?

Page 29 **No American Jew had ever given so much to so many charitable agencies and causes.**
What is a philanthropist? What are some of the ways Judah Touro expressed his philanthropic ideals?

Page 30 **One Jewish woman..., Josephine Sarah Marcus, gained a place among the legends of the Wild West...**
Few people know that Wyatt Earp, the famous lawman and gunfighter, was married to Josephine Marcus. At the end of his life he was laid to rest in a Jewish cemetery.

Page 31 **Wherever they went, the pattern of Jewish settlement remained basically the same.**
Find out about the founding of your community. Did it follow a pattern similar to the one described in the text? Were the early Jewish settlers mainly merchants, traders, and peddlers? Why were these logical professions for new Jewish immigrants to enter?

Page 32 **The First Jewish Commodore**
What personal qualities did Uriah Phillips Levy display? Did these qualities help him to be a success? Why or why not? How are his views concerning the balance of justice and mercy reflective of Jewish ideals?

Page 33 **The peddler's life was not easy.**
A peddler had to buy a license to do business in each state that he traveled in. This license was often quite expensive and made it even more difficult to earn a profit. Describe the life of a rural peddler. What were some of the positive and negative qualities of this life? Why did most Jews not remain peddlers for very long?

Page 34 **Other German Jews**
Many German immigrants became quite wealthy. What are some of the ways they used their newly made fortunes to help others? What Jewish value does this behavior reflect?

Jewish Value to Explore

▶ **Tzedakah:** The act of "doing the right thing." Many of the early German Jewish immigrants became wealthy and chose to use part of their fortunes in charitable ways. Jews not only gave money, but shared their time and skills. Many also used their ingenuity to create inventions for the good of all people.

▶ **The balance of *hesed* and *rachamim*:** The balancing of justice and mercy is reflected in many ways in our Jewish tradition. We value the pursuit of justice, but we also recognize the need to show mercy. This concept later came into American law through the U.S. Constitution, which states that there shall be no "cruel or unusual punishment."

Suggested Activities

1. Pretend you are a young person who has traveled to California in search of gold. Write home to your family and describe your trip and your experiences upon arriving in California. Include your manner of travel, experiences along the way, and what life is like in California. Remember, everything is very expensive and there is not much law and order. There are so many Jews in your situation, however, that you all get together for services on Yom Kippur. Do you strike it rich?

2. Choose one of the personalities described in this chapter, and do some extra research to learn a bit more about the person. Dress as your character and have the class interview you for a newspaper article on successful American Jews.

3. Make a chart of all the people mentioned in this chapter and their contributions to life in America. Use this information to play a Jeopardy style game where the leader reads a fact and the student must guess the name associated with it. For homework, the students can each write five questions that they can use in the game.

4. Imagine that you a wealthy immigrant. You would like to use a portion of your fortune to help others. What would you choose to do with your money? Explain the reasons for your choices.

Discussion Questions

1. Describe the life of a peddler. Why did so many Jews turn to this line of work? Why were peddlers needed? What were some of the professions Jews chose to move on to as they became more successful?

2. What were some of the factors that motivated Jews to travel west?

3. What product made Levi Strauss famous?

4. Who were some important Jewish philanthropists? What are some of the projects that made them famous? What motivated them to develop these projects?

Further Research Possibilities

1. Research the source of your family name. Was it changed? If so, what was the original name? What reasons does your family give for the change? What about your mother's family name?

2. Is there a hospital, library, school, museum, or other institution that was founded by German Jewish immigrants of the 1800s in your community? If so, find out more about the institution.

Primary Source Worksheet

Photocopy the black line master on the next page in the quantity you require and distribute a copy to each student. After your students have read the proclamation, pose these questions:

1. Where did Mordecai Manuel Noah plan to create a Jewish city of refuge? Why do you think he called it Ararat?

2. Why did Noah think that a city of refuge for Jews was a good idea? Do you agree? List some of the advantages and disadvantages.

3. Would you have gone to live there? Why or why not?

4. The idea of an island of refuge for Jews was a failure. No one came. Why do you think this was the case?

PRIMARY SOURCE MATERIAL

▶ On September 25, 1825, Mordecai Manual Noah, one of the best-known Jews of his generation, proposed to create "a city of refuge for the Jews" on an island in the Niagara River near Buffalo, New York. This is part of his proclamation.

Therefore, I, Mordecai Manuel Noah, have issued this my Proclamation, announcing to the Jews throughout the world, that an asylum is prepared and hereby offered to them, where they can enjoy that peace, comfort and happiness which have been denied them through the intolerance and misgovernment of former ages; an asylum in a free and powerful country remarkable for its vast resources, where industry is encouraged, education promoted, "a land of milk and honey," where Israel may repose in peace, under his "vine and fig tree," and where our people may qualify for that great and final restoration to their ancient heritage.

The desired spot in the State of New York, to which I hereby invite my beloved people throughout the world, is called Grand Island, and on which I shall lay the foundation of a City of Refuge, to be called Ararat.

5 The Eastern European Jews Arrive

Let Freedom Ring (pages 36-44)

Chapter Overview

Jews living in Eastern Europe responded to the pogroms of the late 1800s and the dire poverty of their situations by emigrating to America. During this period nearly 2.5 million Jews came to the United States from Russia and the countries of Eastern Europe. Sailing past the Statue of Liberty, which bears the poem of Emma Lazarus, they entered through the gates of Ellis Island, then crowded into the streets of lower Manhattan looking for work.

Many of the German Jews who had arrived a generation before gave a helping hand, donating funds to establish schools where new immigrants could learn English and the values of democracy. Some of the immigrants found paths to fame and fortune through sports and through the entertainment field.

Important Events Your Students Will Witness

- **The pogroms of 1881 and 1903:** Mobs of peasants organized attacks against the homes and businesses of Jews living in Eastern Europe. Police merely looked on as peasants rampaged through towns and villages, claiming that the Jews were responsible for all their troubles.

- **Mass immigration to the United States:** Between 1881 and 1924 more than 2.5 million Jews came to the United States from Eastern Europe.

Places Your Students Will Visit

- **Ellis Island:** Where new immigrants were examined and processed before being allowed to enter the mainland of the United States.

- **New York's Lower East Side:** Where many of the new immigrants lived and worked in very crowded conditions.

People Your Students Will Meet Along the Way

- **Emma Lazarus:** Poet whose poem about coming to America is inscribed at the base of the Statue of Liberty.

- **Sholom Aleichem:** The famous Yiddish writer who returned to Europe after only a brief stay in America. He preferred the scholarly life of European Jewry to the raw, undignified *life of American Jews*.

- **Henrietta Szold:** Woman who organized classes for new immigrants in Baltimore, Maryland. She also founded Hadassah, the Women's Zionist Organization of America.

- **Benny Leonard, Ruby Goldstein and Barney Ross:** Famous Jewish boxers of the 1920s.
- **Irving Berlin, George Gershwin, Lee Shubert, Fanny Brice, Zero Mostel, and Jerome Kern:** Famous Jews in the entertainment field.

Important Dates
- **1882:** The Russians issued "The May Laws," which forced Jews to leave small villages and towns in which they had lived for generations and move to cities.
- **1881, 1903–1906:** These were the years of documented pogroms in Russia.
- **1893:** Rabbi Israel Meir Ha-Cohen ruled against migration to America.

Terms Your Students Will Be Able to Define
- **Pogroms:** Organized massacres of helpless people.
- **Migration:** A movement of people (or animals) from one land area to another.

Introducing the Lesson

Imagine you are a young person, age fourteen, from a reasonably well-off family in Russia. Your older brother saves up and buys himself a ticket on a steamship heading for America. He is ready to leave when he falls in love with a local girl who will not leave her family in order to marry him and accompany him to America. He doesn't know what to do. Finally he decides to stay in Russia and marry his sweetheart. He offers the ticket to you.

If you choose to go to America, you will have to travel alone. You will have to say goodbye to your family and friends forever. You may never see them again. When you get to America, you will not know anyone. One the other hand, excitement, adventure, and the prospect of a successful future could be yours.

Ask the class, "What would you do?" Let this discussion lead into the topic of Eastern European immigration and what it was like to be a new immigrant on the Lower East Side of New York at the turn of the century.

(This is the true story of my grandmother Lena, who came to America by herself when she was fourteen. She never saw her family again, but she married, raised a family, worked in a shirtwaist factory, and learned English in the evenings. Her brother and the rest of the family who stayed in Europe died in the Holocaust.)

Teaching Opportunities in the Text

Page 37 The Jewish Response
The Jews of Russia responded to persecution and poverty in several different ways. Some became Zionists, some became communists, some clung to the old synagogue communities, and some came to America. If you had to make such a choice, which option would you choose? Why? What happened to many of those who chose to remain in Europe?

Page 37 The Jewish immigrants crossed the Atlantic on steamships... .
The trip across the ocean was an arduous one. Conditions aboard ship were crowded and unsanitary. Food and water were limited and of poor quality. Many

got terribly seasick and some died of diseases. If they had known in advance of the hardships, would immigrants still have undertaken the voyage?

Page 38 **Most of the rabbis of Eastern Europe refused to go to America... .**
Many of the European rabbis not only refused to come to America, they counseled their followers not to go. What reasons did they give for this decision? In your opinion were they right?

Page 39 **...the immigrant was sent back to Europe.**
All new immigrants were examined by doctors as they entered Ellis Island. If you were an immigrant found to have some sort of unacceptable medical condition, the doctor would place a large chalk letter on your coat and you would be pulled aside for deportation. You would be placed on the next ship returning to the port from which you came. Children were allowed to travel with a parent, but if you were ten or older you would be sent back alone, to arrive at a strange port city, not knowing a soul.

It was common to see a family huddled to the side, trying to decide if their unwell family member should travel home alone or if the entire family should return together. Imagine being in this situation. What might your family decide?

Page 40 **Immigrant Life**
New immigrants found every aspect of life challenging. Work, school, home, language, food, clothing, all presented difficulties that had to be overcome. Discuss what some of these challenges were, and the strategies that were used to overcome them.

Page 40–41 **(The Photographs)**
A picture is worth a thousand words. Have your students examine these photographs. What clues do you see as to what life was like for the new immigrants in the large American cities?

Page 42 **Helping the New Immigrants**
Name some of the organizations that were founded to help new immigrants adjust to life in America. What were some of the services they performed?

Page 43 **Pathways to Fame and Fortune**
New immigrants found their way to fame and riches through sports, entertainment, and sometimes crime. Why are these common paths for a new immigrant to take?

Jewish Value to Explore

▶ **Helping people to help themselves:** Maimonides explains that we give *tzedakah* in many ways. We might feel obligated and give grudgingly. We may give freely but want our names to be associated publicly with the gift.

Maimonides places eight of these variations on the rungs of a ladder and teaches us that we should work toward moving from the lowest to the highest rung. On the lowest rung we give small amounts and unwillingly. On the highest rung we give so that the receiver can then become self-sufficient. (See page 51 of the text).

The Jewish organizations that formed at the turn of the century were designed to do just that. They offered all sorts of aid and assistance to new immigrants that was specifically designed to help each individual become a successful and productive member of American society.

Suggested Activities

1. Have the class read more about the life of Sholom Aleichem from encyclopedia articles or from a biography. Discuss his life and works. Read one of Sholom Aleichem's short stories and discuss. What sort of writer was he? In what language did he write? Why was he so popular?

2. Pretend you are Emma Lazarus and you wish to win a contest by writing a poem about coming to America. Have the members of the class write contest entries. Draw a large poster of the Statue of Liberty and inscribe some of the poems at the base. Take a moment to look at the full version of Emma Lazarus' poem.

3. Find other books that contain photographs of Jewish immigrants coming to America or living in America. Share and discuss.

4. Read more about the life of Henrietta Szold. Prepare short essays about her life and works.

5. Suggest that the students view movies such as *Hester Street*, *Fiddler on the Roof*, or *Funny Girl*, the story of Fanny Brice.

6. If you are in the vicinity of Ellis Island or the Statue of Liberty, organize a field trip to the museums at these historic sites.

Discussion Questions

1. What were the factors that motivated many Eastern European Jews to come to America?

2. What were some of the alternative responses some Jews made to the difficult situation in Europe?

3. Why did many of the Eastern European rabbis warn their followers not to go to America?

4. Describe the arrival procedure at Ellis Island. What must it have felt like to arrive there as a new immigrant?

5. What were some of the challenges that faced new immigrants on the Lower East Side of Manhattan at the turn of the century? How did they attempt to cope with these challenges?

6. What were some of the Jewish organizations that helped new immigrants adjust to life in America? What were some of the services they provided?

7. What were some of the professions that enabled new immigrants to rise quickly to fame and fortune in America?

Further Research Possibilities

Have the students investigate their own family history. When did their family come to America? From which country? Where did they land? Are there any interesting stories the family tells about the experience? When this information is collected, each child should choose a person to play-act in the following scene:

Your classroom is the deck of a steamer ship on its way to America. You have been at sea for two weeks and have one more week to travel before you arrive. You are all bored, hungry, and thirsty and looking forward to the conclusion of the trip. As a means of passing the time, you each tell your story (who you are, where you are from, why you are traveling, etc.). Include any interesting anecdotes the children uncover from their own family's past.

Primary Source Worksheet

Photocopy the black line master on the next page in the quantity you require and distribute a copy to each student. After your students have read the description, ask them to pretend:

It is you who walks up the stairs toward the doctor. You are with your elderly mother and you are concerned that she might not pass the physical examination. Write a paragraph that expresses your thoughts at this moment of your life. How are you feeling after the long ocean voyage? Are you confused and afraid? Are you optimistic about your new life? Who will meet you after your ordeal and welcome you to America? Will your mother be allowed to remain with you, and will you be able to care for her in the New World?

PRIMARY SOURCE MATERIAL

► This account describes one immigrant experience on Ellis Island in the early 1900s. Immigrants were given medical examinations before entering the United States, and those who failed to pass were sent back to Europe. A parent had to accompany any very young child who was deported, but children of ten or older were sent back to Europe alone.

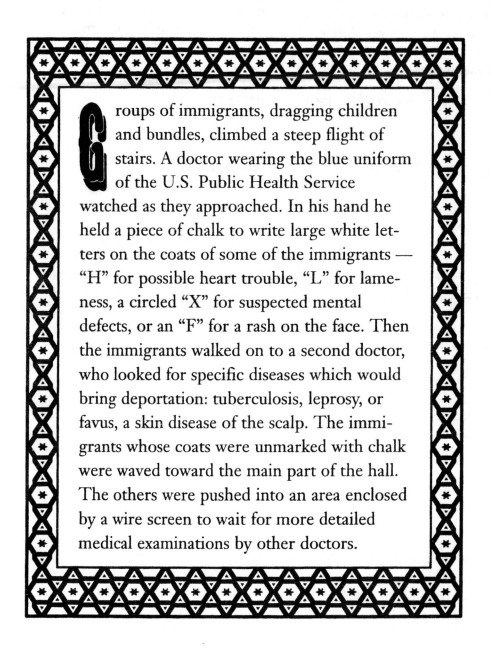

Groups of immigrants, dragging children and bundles, climbed a steep flight of stairs. A doctor wearing the blue uniform of the U.S. Public Health Service watched as they approached. In his hand he held a piece of chalk to write large white letters on the coats of some of the immigrants — "H" for possible heart trouble, "L" for lameness, a circled "X" for suspected mental defects, or an "F" for a rash on the face. Then the immigrants walked on to a second doctor, who looked for specific diseases which would bring deportation: tuberculosis, leprosy, or favus, a skin disease of the scalp. The immigrants whose coats were unmarked with chalk were waved toward the main part of the hall. The others were pushed into an area enclosed by a wire screen to wait for more detailed medical examinations by other doctors.

6 Organizing Jewish Life

Let Freedom Ring (pages 45-52)

Chapter Overview

Jewish life in America did not evolve to follow the same organizational patterns that were set in Eastern Europe. Jews learned to expect choice when it came to religion, and they no longer could agree on such umbrella institutions as a "Chief Rabbinate" or a "Kehillah," a Jewish communal self-government.

Some Jewish organizations in the United States developed in order to protect Jewish rights and fight anti-Semitism. The American Jewish Committee and the Anti-Defamation League of B'nai B'rith are two of these.

Some Jewish organizations evolved as charities to raise money for Jewish causes and needs all over the world. The Joint Distribution Committee raised money for Jews in Europe who had been devastated by World War I. ORT and Hadassah raised money for Jews in Israel. American Jews began to see that they were a chief means of financial support for Jews in need all over the world.

Important Events Your Students Will Witness

- **The founding of the Conservative movement:** Solomon Schechter was brought to America to head the Jewish Theological Seminary. He oversaw the training of rabbis and founded new Conservative synagogues across the United States.
- **The founding of the American Jewish Committee:** This is an organization started by German Jews to "protect Jewish rights wherever they are threatened."
- **World War I:** During this war American Jews raised money to help their brothers and sisters in Europe who were suffering from the devastations of the war.

Places Your Students Will Visit

- **Jewish Theological Seminary of New York:** Where the Conservative movement was born.
- **Boston:** Where the first Jewish federation of charities was established in 1895.

People Your Students Will Meet Along the Way

- **Solomon Schechter:** The person who discovered the Cairo genizah, which contained more than 100,000 manuscripts from Jewish antiquity. He later came to New York and founded the Conservative movement; he built the Jewish Theological Seminary into a thriving rabbinic college.
- **Henry Ford:** The famous automobile manufacturer who promoted anti-Semitism by publishing such hate literature as the *Protocols of the Elders of Zion.*

37

He later retracted some of the hateful things he said and apologized to the Jews for his behavior.

- **Louis Marshall:** One of America's leading lawyers. He fought against the Ku Klux Klan, helped to begin the American Jewish Committee, and defended Leo Frank against false charges of murder.
- **Mordecai M. Kaplan:** Head of the Teacher's Institute of the Jewish Theological Seminary who became the founder of a new branch of Judaism called Reconstructionism.

Important Dates
- **1906:** The America Jewish Committee was founded.
- **1914:** Europe went to war and World War I began.

Terms Your Students Will Be Able to Define
- **Genizah:** A special storage space for keeping worn-out Hebrew books and manuscripts, materials that often contain God's name and therefore should not be destroyed.
- **Hoax:** Something intended to trick, deceive, or defraud.
- **Kehillah:** A Hebrew word meaning community.
- **Federation:** The act of uniting into a league.

Introducing the Lesson

Ask your students to imagine for a moment that they are new immigrants in America. They notice that within their new neighborhood there are several synagogues. (Back in Europe each small town or neighborhood had only one.) One is Orthodox, one is Conservative, one is Reform. In one the prayer is in English, in another Russian, in another Hebrew. They differ in many ways and you can choose to attend any one you wish.

What are some of the important factors that will help you to decide which synagogue you would prefer? How did these types of decisions contribute to the growth of new synagogues in the United States? How did the new concept of freedom of choice affect the growth of synagogues? Is this new "choice" a good thing? How do the synagogues in your community reflect this diversity?

Teaching Opportunities in the Text

Page 45 ....**the idea of uniting under one chief rabbi was abandoned.**
The institution of "Chief Rabbi" was established in many of the countries of Europe and was brought to the State of Israel by the British. Discuss why the concept didn't work in America.

Page 46 **When Solomon Schechter heard about a genizah... .**
Explain what a *genizah* is and its purpose. Why was the *genizah* in Cairo such an important find? What kinds of things were in it? What do you think Solomon Schechter hoped to learn from studying its contents?

Page 47 **The Great Hoax**
The literature of hate is particularly harmful because people tend to believe things that they read in print in magazines, books, and newspapers. Why do you think this is so? Can you name other examples of printed materials that were created for the specific purpose of spreading lies about others? Henry Ford apologized for disseminating this book. How do you feel about his apology?

Page 48 **...they met...and created the American Jewish Committee...**
What was the purpose of this new organization? Why was it necessary in America at that time? Is it still necessary today? Why?

Page 49 **World War I**
In the beginning of our text, we learned how new immigrants to the early colonies had to ask their families and friends in Europe for aid and assistance. Two hundred years later the tables have turned and the American Jewish community is the strong and healthy community that is furnishing aid to the Jews of Europe. Discuss how time and the flow of history change the roles we play in the world, sometimes within a very short period of time.

Page 50 **Organizing Jewish Charities**
What are some of the Jewish fund-raising organizations that exist in your community? Does your city have a federation? What are some of the institutions and organizations that your federation supports?

Page 51 **Tzedakah**
The word *tzedakah* means "righteousness, or doing the right thing." What are some other Hebrew words that use the same root, *tzadik, dalet, koof*?

Tzodek = Correct.
Tzadik = A righteous person, sometimes translated as "saint."
Tzedek = Justice, as in the famous phrase from the Torah, "*Tzedek, tzedek tirdof*" (Justice, justice, you shall pursue).

Page 52 **Kaplan believed in giving women full equality in Judaism.**
Mordecai Kaplan had many new ideas as to how Judaism should be practiced in America. One was to give women equality when it came to Jewish practice. How has this idea progressed since the Bat Mitzvah of Judith Kaplan in 1922? What were some of Mordecai Kaplan's other new ideas?

Jewish Value to Explore

▶ **Tzedakah:** Righteousness.

▶ **Kedushah:** Holiness. Jews consider the four-letter name of God, known as the tetragramaton, to be particularly holy and closely connected with God. We therefore do not destroy books and papers that contain this name. Rather, we keep them in a safe place, known as a *genizah*, for future burial in a cemetery. Ask your rabbi if such a place exists in your synagogue and share the information with your students.

39

Suggested Activities

1. Have your class pretend that they are members of your community's Jewish federation. You collected $100,000 this year in your annual fund-raising campaign. First discuss and select the charities you wish to support. When you have chosen six worthy organizations to support, try to agree as to how much money you wish to give to each this year. Have one student advocate for each organization before the class votes. Conclude by discussing the results. What did you choose? Why? Was it easy to decide? Why or why not? Did your process simulate the reality of your community federation's tasks?

2. Compare the major Jewish movements in the United States: Orthodox, Conservative, Reform, and Reconstructionist. List several of the points that distinguish each as being unique, when they were formed, their major founders, their seminaries, etc. This can be done as a large chart or individually by each child.

3. Read about the famous case of Leo Frank, a Jewish man who was hanged by a lynch mob in Georgia in 1915 for a murder he did not commit. Use this event to spur discussions of discrimination and anti-Semitism in the United States. Discuss cases of discrimination perpetrated against other groups as well. Do these issues still exist for us today? What can we do to fight them?

4. Learn more about the life and career of Louis Marshall or Solomon Schechter. Have students dress in character and report in the first person as to their life and work.

5. Create a large poster of a ladder and label each rung corresponding to Maimonides' famous hierarchy of giving. Have children give concrete examples for each rung and display these on the poster.

Discussion Questions

1. Why did American Orthodox Jews attempt to create an office of "Chief Rabbi" in the United States? Why did this attempt fail?

2. Who was Solomon Schechter? What were his major contributions to the growth of Jewish life in America?

3. What were some of the events that led to the creation of the America Jewish Committee?

4. What was the Kehillah? Why was this not an idea suited for life in America?

5. Why was the Joint Distribution Committee founded? What was its function? How does the founding of this organization show that the role of American Jews had changed in the world?

6. What is the purpose of a Jewish federation and how does it function?

7. What is a *genizah*? Why do we keep such a place?

8. What are some of the important ideas of Mordecai Kaplan? What movement did he found?

9. What can we learn from Maimonides' *tzedakah* ladder?

Further Research Possibilities

1. Learn more about your synagogue's *genizah*. If there is none, ask your rabbi about starting such a project.

2. Find out more about your community's federation, who runs it, how it operates, which organizations it supports. Perhaps you can become more active in the work of your federation.

Primary Source Worksheet

Photocopy the black line master on the next page in the quantity you require and distribute a copy to each student. After your students have read the article, ask them to imagine:

You are a member of the American Jewish Committee. You have received a copy of this article in the mail. It was clipped and sent to you by a group of concerned Jewish citizens in Michigan who ask you to "do something constructive to refute these lies."

Plan a course of action that would help to lessen the effects of such anti-Semitic propaganda. Write a reply to the group of Jewish citizens describing how the Committee plans to deal with this matter.

▶ During the 1920s a series of articles about a "Jewish plot" to take over the world appeared in Henry Ford's newspaper, *The Dearborn Independent*. This is part of one article published in 1921 which claimed that the Hebrew religious hymn *"Eli, Eli"* was an anti-Christian propaganda spread by a secret Jewish organization.

The Dearborn Independent

Now, as to the Jewish religious hymn which is being sung "by request" throughout the country: The name of the hymn is "Eli, Eli"; its base is the first verse of the Twenty-second Psalm, known best in Christian countries as the Cry of Christ on the Cross.

It is being used by Jewish vaudeville managers as their contribution to the pro-Jewish campaign which the Jew-controlled theater is flinging into the faces of the public, from stage and motion picture screen. It is an incantation designed to inflame the lower classes of Jews against the people, and intensify the racial consciousness of those hordes of Eastern Jews who have flocked here.

At the instigation of the New York Kehillah, "Eli, Eli" has for a long time been sung at the ordinary run of performances in vaudeville and motion picture houses, and the notice "By Request" is usually a bald lie. It should be "By Order." The "request" is from Jewish headquarters which has ordered the speeding up of Jewish propaganda. The situation of the theater now is that American audiences are paying at the box office for the privilege of hearing Jews advertise the things they want non-Jews to think about them. This Yiddish chant is the rallying cry of race hatred which is being spread abroad by orders of the Jewish leaders.

"Eli, Eli" is not a religious hymn! It is a racial war cry.

7 The Labor Movement

Let Freedom Ring (pages 53-60)

Chapter Overview

By the turn of the century many of the new Jewish immigrants to the United States were working in garment industry factories, particularly in New York City. Wages were low, working conditions were poor, and the workday was very long. The abuses perpetrated upon workers by the industry management led to the rise of the labor movement and labor unions. Many of these organizations had a large Jewish constituency and Jewish leadership. After numerous strikes, and tragedies such as the Triangle Shirtwaist fire, these unions were successful in improving working conditions and wages for many American workers.

Many in the American rabbinate, such as Stephen S. Wise, championed causes of social justice and social reform. They joined the labor unions in fighting for the freedom and well-being of American workers.

Important Events Your Students Will Witness

- **The uprising of the twenty thousand:** A major strike led by the International Ladies' Garment Workers' Union in 1909, which resulted in a history-making settlement negotiated by Louis Brandeis.

- **The Triangle Shirtwaist fire of 1911:** In which 146 workers died, trapped by flames and smoke on the top story of a sweatshop in New York City. The fire called public attention to the poor working conditions in factories such as this one.

Places Your Students Will Visit

- **The sweatshops of New York City:** Where many new immigrants worked after arriving in America. Pay was low, and conditions were poor. These unsatisfactory conditions gave rise to labor discontent and the beginnings of the labor movement.

People Your Students Will Meet Along the Way

- **Samuel Gompers:** A Jewish labor leader who became the president of what would soon become the American Federation of Labor. He fought for the eight-hour workday, worked for child labor laws, and organized health centers and schools for workers.

- **Morris Hillquit:** Organizer of the United Hebrew Trades, an umbrella organization for all working Jews.

- **Clara Lemlich:** Leader of a shirtwaist makers' strike.

- **Louis D. Brandeis:** A Boston Jewish lawyer who helped negotiate an end to the ILGWU strike of 1909. He later became a member of the U.S. Supreme Court.
- **Sidney Hillman and David Dubinsky:** Famous Jewish labor leaders.
- **Abraham Cahan:** Founder and editor of the Yiddish newspaper the *Jewish Daily Forward* from 1902 to 1951.
- **Stephen S. Wise:** American Reform rabbi who was known for his work in the area of human rights. He was the founder of the Free Synagogue of New York.

Important Dates
- **1907:** The Free Synagogue was founded in New York City.
- **1935:** Congress passed the National Labor Relations Act, which gave workers the right to organize and required employers to bargain with labor unions.

Terms Your Students Will Be Able to Define
- **Strike:** To stop work as a means of financial coercion.
- **Negotiate:** To deal with or discuss with another in preparation for a settlement.
- **Yiddish:** The language of many of the Jews of Eastern Europe. It is a mixture of German and Hebrew.

Introducing the Lesson

What was it like to work in a sweatshop in New York City? Ask the class to imagine what it would be like to work in a dimly lit and dirty basement — poorly ventilated so it is too hot in the summer and too cold in the winter — to work there day after day from 7:00 A.M. until 8:00 P.M. How would you feel knowing that if you complained you would be immediately fired and would have no money to support your family? What would your life be like?

Explain that this chapter is about the lives of Jewish workers and the methods they used to improve their working conditions and wages.

Teaching Opportunities in the Text

Page 53 **Sweatshop pay was very low....**
Why were so many of the new immigrants forced to work for such low pay and in such terrible conditions? Does this still occur when new immigrants come to our country today?

Page 54 **When he saw the poverty and misery and suffering in the sweatshop, he thought of how the Bible hated slavery.**
What part of the Bible do you think Gompers was referring to? What famous Jewish hero does he remind you of? (Moses and the Exodus from Egypt. Moses could not bear to see his fellow Jews suffer under the yoke of Egyptian oppression.)

Page 55 **Hillquit's strike was a success.**
What were the ingredients that went into creating a successful strike? What were some things that might happen that could cause a strike to fail?

Page 56 **The Uprising of the Twenty Thousand**
Industrialization changed the lives of women forever. For the first time in history, women were working outside their homes in great numbers. In 1909 thousands of women fought for their rights in the workplace and led a successful strike that became a model for others to come. The women in the picture on page 56 will still have to wait eleven years until the passage of the Nineteenth Amendment to the Constitution, which will grant them the right to vote. How were the lives of women changed by their entry into the work force?

Page 57 **The "Bintel Brief"**
The *Jewish Daily Forward* served the Jewish community of New York City for years. Why do you think it was so popular? Why did Jews need their own newspaper along with the other English newspapers? Is a Jewish newspaper published in your community? What is its name? What kinds of news and articles does it print? Does it have an "advice" column like the "Bintel Brief"?

Page 58 **The Triangle Shirtwaist Fire**
The fire brought many of the issues of working people to the attention of the general public. What were some of these issues? Do you think that the fire caused society to make any lasting changes in dealing with these issues?

Page 59 **A Rabbi for All Seasons**
Rabbi Stephen S. Wise was known for his work in all areas of human rights. List some of the issues he was involved with. What do all these issues have in common?

Page 60 **Social justice has always been an important value in Judaism.**
The labor movement and religious Jews share many common values. What values do they share? The phrase, "Justice, justice you shall pursue" comes from the book of Deuteronomy. Discuss the meaning of this phrase.

Jewish Value to Explore

▶ **Zecher yetziat Mitzraim:** Remember the going out from Egypt. We remember our experiences as slaves in Egypt each time we recite the *kiddush* over wine, and each Passover as we read the haggadah. As Jews, when we remember leaving Egypt, we remember slavery, hardship, and oppression. Each of us carries that memory for all time, and when we see hurt and oppression suffered by others in the world, we are commanded to act. We are commanded by our memory to work for human rights everywhere in the world, as did Samuel Gompers and other Jewish labor leaders of the early 1900s.

Suggested Activities

1. The *Jewish Daily Forward* was a Yiddish newspaper. Yiddish, which was the language of many Eastern European Jews, is a mix of German and Hebrew. Listen to a recorded Yiddish song or poem to hear the sound of the language. You might be able to invite someone who speaks Yiddish to class to make a presentation.

2. Many labor laws in the United States are a result of the work of labor leaders from the early 1900s. We have a minimum wage and standards for working conditions, benefits, and the length of the workday. Because of these, many manufacturers choose to take their industries overseas, where labor is cheap and labor laws don't exist. Have your students research more on this issue and share their views.

3. Learn more about Samuel Gompers, Stephen Wise, or Louis Brandeis. Dress as your character and present your research to the class.

4. Pretend that you are Clara Lemlich advocating a strike of the shirtwaist makers' union. Prepare your speech and deliver it to the class.

5. You are a young woman and a new immigrant in America. You are the first woman in your family to work outside the home. Write a letter to your mother in Europe describing your life. Compare your life to hers.

6. You are all members of the cigar makers' union and it is time to choose a new president. Choose two candidates to present themselves and their platform. Have the class elect a president.

7. The factory you work in has a 13-hour workday. Pay is low and working conditions are unsanitary. Your union president feels you should go on strike. After several days of picketing, you choose a negotiating committee to meet with the factory owners. Louis Brandeis, the lawyer, is also present to help you work out an agreement.

   Each side should list the issues that are most important to them. They should be in order of importance, with the most important first. Each side should plan a negotiating strategy. Create negotiating ground rules. Reenact the negotiations as they might truly occur in this situation. Try to come to a contractual agreement within a time frame chosen by the teacher. Discuss the results.

8. Look at the issues with which Stephen Wise became involved (page 59). How many are still with us today? Choose one that may have some local impact on your community and plan a course of action that your class can follow to do their part in improving the human condition. You might raise funds, write letters to a newspaper, prepare food packages, etc.

Discussion Questions

1. What is a sweatshop? How did it get its name?

2. List some of the industries Jews were involved in as new immigrants to the United States at the turn of the twentieth century.

3. Who was Samuel Gompers and what were some of his major accomplishments? In what way was he affected by his Jewish studies.

4. What was the purpose of creating the United Hebrew Trades?

5. What was the *Jewish Daily Forward?* Why was it important?

6. How did the Triangle Shirtwaist fire educate the American public about the problems of sweatshop workers?

7. Describe the work of Stephen S. Wise. How did he connect his work as a rabbi with his work as a social reformer?

8. How did Jewish teachings shape the attitudes of Jewish labor leaders in the United States?

Further Research Possibilities

1. Find out if any members of your family worked in factories or sweatshops. Were any of them members of labor unions? If members of your family have interesting stories to tell, share them with the class. For example, my grandfather Jack was one of the original leaders of the Electrical Workers Union in New York City. He tells me that it was so dangerous to be a union leader in those days that he had to carry a gun. He is very proud of his part in the organization of the union.

2. Research what some of our current labor laws are today. What is the current minimum wage? What are some of the laws regarding child labor? Can you work if you want to? How old do you have to be to get a job? What are some of our current laws regarding safety on the job, health care, and child care? Remember that all these new laws are the result of the work done by people like Samuel Gompers and Clara Lemlich.

....

Primary Source Worksheet

Photocopy the black line master on the next page in the quantity you require and distribute a copy to each student. After your students have read the speech, ask them to do the following:

Using the information in the chapter and in Rose Schneiderman's speech, write an article to appear in the *Jewish Daily Forward* on March 26, 1911 — the day after the Triangle fire.

Or write a letter to the editor to suggest things that should be changed after this terrible event.

PRIMARY SOURCE MATERIAL

▶ In 1911 Rose Schneiderman, a leader in the Hat and Cap Makers' Union, gave a speech about the need for workers to organize and protect themselves from tragedies such as the fire at the Triangle Shirtwaist Company. These are some of the things she said.

I would be a traitor to these poor burned bodies if I came here to talk good fellowship. This is not the first time girls have been burned alive in the city. Every week I must learn of the untimely death of one of my sister workers. Every year thousands of us are maimed. The life of men and women is so cheap and property is so sacred. There are so many of us for one job, it matters little if 146 of us are burned to death.

We have tried you citizens, we are trying you now, and you have a couple of dollars for the sorrowing mothers, brothers, and sisters by way of a charity gift. But every time the workers come out in the only way they know to protest against conditions which are unbearable, the strong hand of the law is allowed to press down heavily upon us.

Public officials have only words of warning to us — warning that we must be intensely peaceable, and they have the workhouse just back of their warnings. The strong hand of the law beats us back, when we rise, into the conditions that make life unbearable.

I can't talk fellowship to you who are gathered here. Too much blood has been spilled. I know from my experience it is up to the working people to save themselves. The only way they can save themselves is by a strong working-class movement.

Coming of Age

Let Freedom Ring (pages 61-67)

Chapter Overview

By the twentieth century, American Jews were no longer just trying to "fit in." They were changing the face of science and medicine with new inventions and discoveries. People like Albert Einstein and Jonas Salk were center stage in helping America grow into a mighty nation.

Despite these contributions, Congress began to limit immigration with a new law passed in 1924. The public was pleased with this turn of events. They were afraid of losing jobs to new immigrants and of having too many new Americans to feed. The public perception that many Jews were communists also contributed to the negative feeling. Anti-Semitic activity increased as the great Depression ravaged the country. The land of freedom and opportunity was no longer as welcoming as it once was.

Important Events Your Students Will Witness

- **The Great Depression:** When the stock market crashed in 1929, thousands lost their life savings. The country was plunged into financial disaster almost overnight.

Places Your Students Will Visit

- **Brandeis University:** Established in 1948 to give equal opportunity to all in the area of higher education.

People Your Students Will Meet Along the Way

- **Albert Abraham Michelson:** First American to be awarded the Nobel Prize. He was the first to calculate the speed of light.
- **Joseph Goldberger:** Founder of the modern science of nutrition.
- **Albert Einstein:** Scientist who discovered the theory of relativity.
- **Jonas Salk:** Doctor who developed the anti-polio vaccine.
- **The Rosenwald family:** Developers of Sears Roebuck & Company. They were known as great philanthropists.
- **Louis D. Brandeis:** The first Jew to be appointed to the U.S. Supreme Court.
- **Father Charles E. Coughlin:** Priest who preached anti-Semitism on the radio for years.
- **Henry "Hank" Greenberg:** Famous Jewish baseball player, voted most valuable player in 1935 and 1940. He is also remembered for refusing to play in the pennant race on Yom Kippur.

Important Dates
- **1924:** Congress passed restrictive immigration laws.
- **1929:** The Great Depression began.

Terms Your Students Will Be Able to Define
- **Nobel Prize:** An international award for achievements in the sciences, literature, and other fields.
- **Communism:** A system of social organization based upon the holding of all property in common.

Introducing the Lesson

Starting in the early 1920s, the atmosphere of tolerance that had been a hallmark of our nation began to change. Prejudice and fear replaced hospitality and warmth, and Jews no longer felt welcomed everywhere they went. Immigration laws were passed that greatly reduced the number of Jews allowed to enter the country each year, and Jews were afraid to speak out against these laws.

Ask your students to imagine that they are recent immigrants to America in 1924. New laws were just passed that cut Jewish immigration, and their parents, who still live in Poland, cannot come to America to join them, as they had planned. What do they do? Should they speak out? Why or why not? What are their choices?

As the students suggest options, try to inform them as to what might have been the reality of trying that course of action in 1924. At the end of the discussion ask them how they feel. Is there a sense of frustration or anger at the lack of justice? How must this turn of events have really felt to those living at that time?

Teaching Opportunities in the Text

Page 62 **Jewish Contributions to Science and Medicine**
Can you think of other famous Jews who became known for their contributions to the technology of our modern world? Why do we feel it's important to point out that they are Jewish?

Page 63 **The Changing Immigration Laws**
Why were so many people in agreement with these changing laws? What did they fear?

Page 63 **Some Jews — especially those who were part of the labor movement — had joined the American Communist Party.**
What is communism? Why do you think some Jews were attracted to this ideology?

Page 64 **The Rosenwald Family**
Why do you think the Rosenwald family chose the Tuskegee Institute and the support of black schools in the south as the main focus of their *tzedakah?*

What Jewish values does this action express? What part of the Jewish past must have been in their memory?

Page 64 **There was also discrimination against Jews in hiring ....**
What are some of the safeguards our society has created so that these sorts of practices no longer happen?

Page 65 **The Great Depression**
How did the onset of the Depression cause prejudice and discrimination to increase? What were some of the daily stresses that people had to face during these hard time?

Page 66 **Now the Jewish hospitals became places where new Jewish doctors could practice their trade.**
Why was it necessary for the Jewish community to found their own hospitals and law firms? Do some of these still exist today? Has their role changed?

Page 67 **A Baseball Great**
Why does the text stress the fact that Hank Greenberg and Sandy Koufax refused to play ball on Jewish holidays? How does their decision affect you?

Jewish Value to Explore

▶ **Tzedek:** The Torah teaches us, "Justice, justice you shall pursue." The founding of Brandeis University in 1948 was an attempt by the Jewish community to counteract discrimination and prejudice. The Jews created a university based on the principle of equal opportunity to all.

▶ **Talmud Torah:** Jewish tradition and culture place great value on study, learning, and knowledge. The most revered member of a Jewish community was the one who was the most learned. This attitude is reflected in secular studies as well as in religious studies. The number of great Jewish doctors and scientists, as well as the many Jewish men and women who have distinguished themselves in other professions, is a reflection of this value in our culture.

Suggested Activities

1. Choose a famous Jewish doctor or scientist and research his or her life and work. Create a short presentation for the class based on your findings. The teacher might wish to create a list of names for the class to choose from.

2. Standardized tests were used in court to discredit Jews in 1924 (see page 63 of the text). Have the students discuss their experiences with standardized tests. Are these tests fair? Do they accurately judge performance? What sorts of judgments should we base upon their results? What sorts of judgments might be unfair?

3. Have the class prepare a debate on the question, "Should the United States limit immigration from foreign countries?" This was an issue in 1924 and

continues today. Choose sides and have each group come in prepared to discuss the issues.

4. Prejudice and discrimination have been a part of American life for a long time. Jews were victims of it in the past and occasionally still experience it today. Other minority groups also have suffered from discrimination. Have your students list the areas of life that can be affected by prejudice or discriminatory practices. Next to each item on the list try to list a remedy in use today. If none exists, suggest possible solutions.

5. Have your students write or tell about a time when they had a conflict between an activity and a Jewish holiday. How was that conflict resolved? Would you do it differently if you had it to do over? How does your resolution compare with that of Hank Greenberg and Sandy Koufax? What do you think of their choice? Why?

Discussion Questions

1. By the twentieth century new immigrants were making an impact on what it meant to be an American. Who were some of these people and what were their accomplishments?

2. What does it mean to limit immigration? What are some of the motivations for such a policy?

3. What were some of the specific reasons that were given for limiting Jewish immigration?

4. Why were Jews afraid of speaking out against this policy?

5. What famous business did the Rosenwald family develop? What famous institution did they choose to support with the fortune they made?

6. Why were Jews kept from advancement in business? Why did many Jewish doctors and lawyers find it difficult to practice their profession?

7. What were some of the changes people suffered during the Great Depression? How did these changes affect Jews in particular?

8. Hank Greenberg and Sandy Koufax both refused to play ball on Yom Kippur. Why are these two events important for Jews to remember?

Further Research Possibilities

1. Ask your grandparents if they remember what life was like in America during the Depression. Share these stories with the class.

2. Ask your grandparents if they were ever the victims of any of the types of discrimination described in this chapter. Collect these stories and share them with the group.

Primary Source Worksheet

Photocopy the black line master on the next page in the quantity you require and distribute a copy to each student. After your students have read the excerpt, pose these questions:

1. What did Koufax mean when he said, "There was never any decision to make"?

2. Many people considered Don Riley's newspaper column anti-Semitic. How did Sandy Koufax handle the incident? How would you have handled the same situation?

3. Sandy Koufax's decision not to pitch was a public decision as well as a private one. Sometimes when our Jewish actions are perceived by the public, we make a larger statement than we may have originally planned. How did Koufax's actions affect others? Does his decision still affect us today?

4. What are some of the opportunities you have to make Jewish decisions that have public as well as private consequences? How would your decisions in these situations affect others?

PRIMARY SOURCE MATERIAL

▶ Sandy Koufax, a pitcher for the Los Angeles Dodgers, faced a dilemma. His team had made it to the 1965 World Series and the first game against the Minnesota Twins was scheduled to be played on Yom Kippur. Would he play that day? Sandy Koufax wrote about making the decision in his autobiography.

I had ducked a direct answer about the World Series because it seemed presumptuous to talk about it while we were still trying to get there.... There was never any decision to make, though, because there was never any possibility that I would pitch. Yom Kippur is the holiest day of the Jewish religion. The club knows that I don't work that day.

The surprise of the day, as far as I was concerned, came the next morning when I was reading the report of the game by Don Riley, the columnist of the St. Paul Pioneer Press. His column took the form of "An Open Letter to Sandy Koufax," in which he was kind enough to tell me how badly we had been beaten in the opener and to warn me of the terrible things that lay in store for me.... I found it vastly amusing. Until right at the end. "And the Twins love matzoh balls on Thursday."

I couldn't believe it. I thought that kind of thing went out with dialect comics. I clipped the column so that I could send it back to him after we defeated the Twins with a friendly little notation that I hoped his words were as easy to eat as my matzoh balls.

I didn't, of course. We were winners. The winners laugh, drink champagne, and give the losers the benefit of all doubts.

The Holocaust Years

Let Freedom Ring (pages 68-74)

Chapter Overview

Adolph Hitler rose to power in Germany preaching a new form of anti-Semitism. Immigration was limited in the nations of the west and many Jews found themselves trapped in Europe, where Hitler was preparing the "final solution." Rumors of death camps spread through America, and while many prominent Jewish leaders protested and asked President Roosevelt to rescue the Jews of Europe, little was done. When the war ended, American Jews were shocked to learn that 6 million Jews had been murdered!

Important Events Your Students Will Witness

- **World War II:** War in which the Allied powers fought the Axis powers of Germany, Japan, and Italy to keep the world free of dictatorship.

Places Your Students Will Visit

- **Pre-war Germany:** Where anger and frustration over the results of World War I and the economic depression allowed for the rise of Hitler and his policies of anti-Semitism.

- **Washington, D.C.:** Where frustrated groups of American Jews tried to convince the president to intervene on behalf of the Jews of Europe.

People Your Students Will Meet Along the Way

- **Adolf Hitler:** The Nazi dictator of Germany.

- **Felix Frankfurter:** U.S. Supreme Court Justice who was a friend of President Roosevelt. His attempts to convince the president to help the Jews of Europe were unsuccessful.

- **Anne Frank:** The Dutch Jewish child who became a victim of the Nazis. Her diary depicting these events was found and published for all to read.

- **Elie Wiesel:** Holocaust survivor whose eloquent books describe his experiences during World War II.

- **Adolf Eichman:** Nazi war criminal who was captured and tried for his war crimes.

Terms Your Students Will Be Able to Define

- **Genocide:** The intentional murder of a whole cultural group of human beings.

- **Holocaust:** A great fire that destroys all in its path.

- *Shoah:* Sudden collapse or devastation.
- **Final Solution:** Nazi plan to completely destroy the Jewish people.

Introducing the Lesson

The year is 1938. You are a new immigrant in the United States. You live in New York and work in a shirtwaist factory sewing sleeves onto blouses. You have been writing regularly to your cousin who still lives in Germany. Today you receive a letter from her that reads as follows:

> Dear Gerta,
>
> The last two days have been horrible. I have been afraid to leave home and walk the streets. Everywhere there is broken glass. Mobs have been storming the streets, attacking Jewish businesses, looting, burning synagogues, attacking Jews wherever they might be. Thousands of Jews have been arrested and sent away. No one knows where they have been taken. There is no one who can stop this. There is no voice of reason to be heard. This is no way to live. I hope to come to join you in America soon. As soon as my papers arrive, I will leave this place.
>
> Your cousin,
> Helen

Your cousin was describing the fateful events of November 1938 that came to be known as *Kristallnacht*, "Night of the broken glass." Even though you wrote back, this was the last letter you received from your cousin. One year goes by and you don't hear from her. How do you feel? What do you think has happened? What can you do about it?

Teaching Opportunities in the Text

Page 68 **He preached that Germany had been betrayed by Communists and Jews.**
When people are in trouble, they seem to need to assign blame, even when that blame is falsely placed. Hitler did this by claiming that the Jews were the cause of Germany's problems. He turned the Jews into scapegoats. What is a scapegoat? Where does the image of a scapegoat come from? (See Leviticus 16.) Can you name other times in history when people were unjustly made into scapegoats?

Page 69 **Nazi Anti-Semitism**
Discuss the reasons why it was difficult, if not impossible, to flee from Nazi persecution.

Page 70 **The Final Solution**
The Nazis were scientific and methodical in the manner in which they implemented the "Final Solution." They used their knowledge of technology and their organizational skills to create a death machine more efficient than the world had ever known. The Nazis were learned and knowledgeable, but immoral. Lead a

discussion of how intellectual knowledge, while valued, can be used for both good and evil. Being smart isn't enough. Even more important than intellect are moral values.

Page 72 Did American Jews Do All They Could?

This is a painful question to address. While it is easy to be critical in hindsight, it is necessary to try to put ourselves in the place of American Jews living at that time in order to consider it properly. Ask your students their feelings on this issue. Remind them that Jews of that era did not feel empowered as Americans. They were often the victims of discrimination themselves. Did Americans of the 1940s expect less from their government than we do today?

Page 73 After the Holocaust

Holocaust survivors did not tell their stories right away. It took years before these victims were able to begin talking and writing about their experiences. Why do you think this is so?

Jewish Value to Explore

▶ **Reshit hochma yirat Hashamayim (Proverbs):** Wisdom begins with a fear of Heaven. It is not enough just to be smart. We have to live our lives knowing that God is watching the way we act toward others. Torah teaches us to be aware of the consequences of all our actions and to behave accordingly. The Nazi experience teaches us that knowledge without morality and values should never be our goal.

Suggested Activities

1. Offer a reading list to your students of books about the Holocaust. You might ask each child to choose one and write a book report. Some possible choices are *The Diary of Anne Frank* by Anne Frank, *Night* by Elie Wiesel, *Number The Stars* by Lois Lowry, and *A Place to Hide* by Jayne Pettit. There are many others as well. The students might also be able to share some titles with each other.

2. Several questions come to mind that can be used for discussion, essays, or debates:

   A. How has Jewish life today been affected by the experience of the Holocaust?

   B. What has the world learned from the Holocaust?

   C. How has the world been affected by the experience of the Holocaust?

3. A Christian friend once said to me, "The Holocaust happened fifty years ago. It's in the past. You forgive the Germans for what they did, don't you?" Ask your students how they would respond if someone said this to them.

4. Imagine that you are an American rabbi during the Holocaust years. Write a letter to President Roosevelt expressing your views on what American policy should be toward the Jews of Europe.

Discussion Questions

1. What conditions in Germany allowed Hitler to come to power?

2. What were Hitler's goals for Germany?

3. What was meant by the "final solution"? In what way was this a new form of anti-Semitism?

4. What are some of the ways American Jews tried to help the Jews of Europe? Why were they unsuccessful?

5. How did American Jews finally learn the full impact of the Holocaust on European Jewry? Why did this take so long?

6. Why is it important that we memorialize the experience of the Holocaust? List some of the ways we have done this in America.

Further Research Possibilities

1. Invite a survivor of the Holocaust or a child of a Holocaust survivor to visit your class and share his or her personal experiences.

2. Visit a Holocaust museum, memorial, or exhibit.

Primary Source Worksheet

Photocopy the black line master on the next page in the quantity you require and distribute a copy to each student. After your students have read the speech, pose these questions:

1. What evil did Rabbi Wise see growing in Germany?

2. What do you think he was hoping American Jews would do about it?

3. Was Rabbi Wise fully aware of the extent to which this evil would grow?

4. What was the result of this address? Was he able to mobilize American Jews to help Jews trapped in Europe?

5. Were American Jews able to influence the U.S. government to aid the Jews of Europe?

6. Comment on Rabbi Wise's ability to predict the events of the Holocaust that were to occur within a few years.

PRIMARY SOURCE MATERIAL

▶ On November 24, 1933, Rabbi Stephen S. Wise spoke of the seriousness of the Jewish situation in Germany. These are excerpts from the speech he delivered seven years before the United States entered World War II.

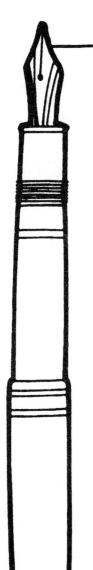

The tragedy of the Jew cannot be stated nor yet summarized in mere facts. And still the truth is that German Jewry presents the picture of a people on the rack. I have seen the torture chamber for the Jewish people.

...The still graver evil is the avowed purpose of Hitlerism, the destruction of world Jewry.

...The formulated and indeed initiated war upon world Jewry is more than cause for alarm to Jews wherever they may dwell. It constitutes the most solemn warning to nations that forces are at work in the world, which are resolved to end understanding between Jew and Christian ... by beginning a crusade against Jews everywhere.

# Opportunities and Challenges

Let Freedom Ring (pages 75-79)

Chapter Overview

Anti-Semitism declined in America at the end of World War II. Jewish soldiers came home ready to build a new future, and America was ready for them. Jews became very successful in many walks of life, including the arts and entertainment. They were pioneers in the new movie and television industry. Many became wealthy. This new prosperous population moved from cities to suburbs, building new communities and synagogues. But despite the fact that 60 percent of Jewish American families belonged to synagogues, religious services were becoming less popular.

Important Events Your Students Will Witness
- **The founding of the first radio and television networks.**
- **The making of the first "talkie" movie:** The Jazz Singer was the story of a young musician whose father was a cantor.

Places Your Students Will Visit
- **Hollywood, California:** Where a new film industry took root.

People Your Students Will Meet Along the Way
- **David Sarnoff:** The man known as the father of television. He founded RCA and NBC.
- **Many famous musicians, actors, movie producers and authors:** Jews who succeeded in all these fields in the years following World War II.

Important Dates
- **1911:** David Sarnoff broadcast the news of the sinking of the Titanic, live, through the first wireless network.

Introducing the Lesson

On the chalkboard list some of the names mentioned on page 78 of the text. Make a second list of their areas of expertise. Add any others you might know. Ask the students how many of these names they recognize. See if they can match the area of expertise with each name. Point out that many Jews became very successful in America after World War II. Lead a discussion about why it was now possible for so many Jews to reach their full potential in America. What had changed?

Teaching Opportunities in the Text

Page 75 **Anti-Semitism continued to decline after the war.**
What factors contributed to this change? Was the same true for other ethnic groups, such as African Americans?

Page 76 **The film industry grew in Hollywood, and the Jews played a major role in shaping it.**
Why do you think Jews became so involved in this new industry from its inception? (While other businessmen already had a foothold in other industries where Jews had been excluded, Jews saw the new movie industry as an opportunity to get in on the ground floor of an industry that would not exclude them. It was a risky business because it was so new. Other established businessmen were less willing to invest because they were already involved in more established businesses.)

Page 77 **The Father of Television**
What were some of the factors that helped to make Sarnoff successful? In what ways did he permanently change life in America?

Page 78 **Success in Entertainment and the Arts**
The people listed on this page became highly successful in their fields because they worked hard and nurtured their talents. Is there something in Judaism that encourages this? Explain.

Page 79 **From Cities to Suburbs**
The freedom of living in America gave Jews the freedom to choose to be religious or not to be religious. Many choose not to observe Jewish law and custom. Some choose religion with great personal fervor. Discuss the many ways in which freedom is affecting the Jewish community in America today.

Jewish Value to Explore

▶ **Kibbud av va-em:** Honor your father and mother (The Fifth Commandment)–It is interesting that the first talking movie, *The Jazz Singer*, is the story of a cantor's son who honors his father and Jewish tradition. He takes his father's place in synagogue on Yom Kippur when his father turns ill, rather than making his own jazz debut. It is a movie where Jewish choices are made. You might ask your students if they think such a movie would be written today. Do you think the main character would still make the same choice if the movie was made today? Why or why not?

Suggested Activities

1. The chapter tells us that after World War II popular culture began to portray Jews in a positive way. TV, movies, radio, and novels showed Jews to be smart, humorous, brave, and respected by others. The way we are portrayed in the media tells us a great deal about what others think of us and what we think of ourselves. Lead a discussion about the portrayal of Jews in the current media. What do these images teach us about the way we are perceived by ourselves and others?

2. Rent a Marx Brothers movie and learn more about this family of Jewish entertainers.

3. David Sarnoff was in on the ground floor of the new radio and television industry. Have the students research more about his life and work and present their findings to the group. Create a video about David Sarnoff's life and work.

4. Have your students use some of the facts and information from this book to create an early radio newscast. Have each child prepare a brief article on various topics from the period. Read them into a tape recorder and then listen to your show.

5. Have the class read a short story by Isaac Bashevis Singer and discuss. The story "Yentl," on which the well-known movie was based, might be a good choice. It is the story of a young Jewish woman who poses as a man in order to be allowed to pursue her studies.

Discussion Questions

1. What were some of the changes that took place in America after World War II that allowed Jews to advance in the professions with greater ease?

2. Life in America has brought freedom and acceptance for Jews. This has been very positive, but also challenging. In what ways can freedom challenge the Jewish way of life?

3. The first talking move, *The Jazz Singer*, expresses traditional Jewish values as well as some of the conflicts that take place when these values come in contact with our secular culture. What are some of the values that the movie expresses? What are some of the pressures or conflicts that the characters face in living out these values?

4. Who was known as "The Father of American Television"? What were some of his accomplishments?

5. Name some of the famous artists, actors, producers, and writers who contributed to the American way of life. List their accomplishments?

6. Statistics show us that fewer and fewer Jewish families are attending synagogue services. Only one-quarter of all Jews keep the dietary laws and only 40 percent of Jews fast on Yom Kippur. Why do you think so few American Jews

choose these traditional Jewish values? Discuss. Perhaps the students would like to write an article for the synagogue bulletin that expresses the results of this discussion.

Further Research Possibilities

Have the students compile a survey that asks questions about the personal observance of their friends and families. Topics such as prayer, Shabbat observance, *kashrut*, *tzedakah*, and holiday observances can be framed into questions of their choice. After they compile a number of completed forms, they should discuss the results and what can be gleaned about their community from the results. The question, "What do the results of our survey tell us about where we are heading as an American Jewish community?" should be the conclusion of the discussion.

Primary Source Worksheet

Photocopy the black line master on the next page in the quantity you require and distribute a copy to each student. After your students have examined the charts, pose these questions:

1. What do these numbers teach us about ourselves? (Remember, our text told us that in the 1960s, 60 percent of Jewish families belonged to synagogues. It is also true that before 1965 only 9 percent of Jewish households were interfaith marriages.)

2. Do you notice any trends?

3. What future challenges do these statistics show?

4. How can we use this information to plan for a healthy Jewish future?

5. What role might you personally play in shaping that future?

▶ In 1990 the Council of Jewish Federations and Welfare Funds (CJF) completed a survey of Jews in the United States. Jewish families were asked questions about intermarriage, synagogue membership, holiday and ritual observance, etc. The resulting statistics give us a picture of how Jews live in America today.

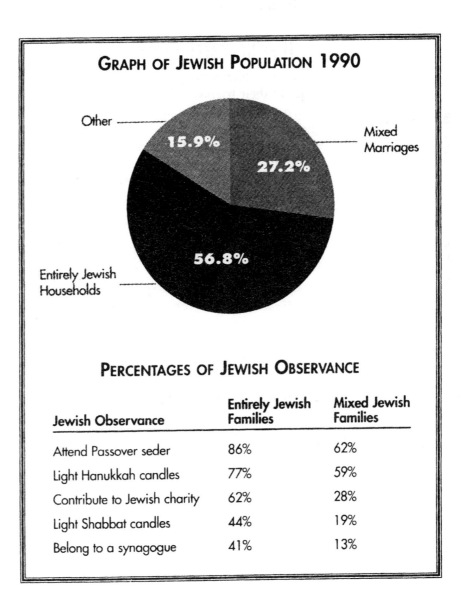

GRAPH OF JEWISH POPULATION 1990

Other — 15.9%

Mixed Marriages — 27.2%

Entirely Jewish Households — 56.8%

PERCENTAGES OF JEWISH OBSERVANCE

Jewish Observance	Entirely Jewish Families	Mixed Jewish Families
Attend Passover seder	86%	62%
Light Hanukkah candles	77%	59%
Contribute to Jewish charity	62%	28%
Light Shabbat candles	44%	19%
Belong to a synagogue	41%	13%

▶ **After you have examined the charts, answer the following questions:**

1. What do these numbers teach us about ourselves? (Remember, our text told us that in the 1960s, 60 percent of Jewish families belonged to synagogues. It is also true that before 1965 only 9 percent of Jewish households were interfaith marriages.)

2. Do you notice any trends?

3. What future challenges do these statistics show?

4. How can we use this information to plan for a healthy Jewish future?

5. What role might you personally play in shaping that future?

11 A New State and a New Agenda

Let Freedom Ring (pages 80-86)

Chapter Overview

As World War II came to a close in Europe, many European Jews found themselves without homes or family. American Jews sent food and clothing and lobbied to increase immigration quotas to the United States, but these efforts weren't enough. All over the world, borders were closed to the refugees.

Some Jews began to make their way to Palestine despite British efforts to institute a blockade. Finally in 1948 the outcry against this British policy was so strong that the United Nations intervened and voted to allow Jews to set up their own independent state in the Middle East.

American Jews were very supportive of this new state. They sent aid and provided loans. Some went to live there. Jews strongly showed their support for the Jewish state also during the wars of 1967 and 1973.

Meanwhile, back in America, Jews were in the forefront of the civil rights movement and active in the peace movement that opposed the war in Vietnam. John F. Kennedy, a Catholic, had been elected president of the United States, the first minority candidate to succeed in this effort. He brought several Jews into his cabinet and, for the first time, showed that the opinions of minorities were important and respected.

Important Events Your Students Will Witness

- **The conclusion of World War II:** As the war ended in 1945, thousands of war victims found themselves destitute, without family or a place to live.
- **The founding of the State of Israel:** The United Nations voted to allow Jews to establish an independent state. Israel's Declaration of Independence was issued and the State of Israel was established.

Places Your Students Will Visit

- **Displaced persons camp:** Where survivors of the Holocaust were placed temporarily after the war. Conditions were difficult. Food was scarce and there were shortages of other necessities.
- **Detention camps:** Where Jews were imprisoned if they were caught trying to sneak into Palestine before 1948.

67

People Your Students Will Meet Along the Way

- **Recha Freier:** The wife of a Berlin rabbi, who began the program of Youth Aliyah.
- **Henrietta Szold:** The founder of Hadassah medical organization.
- **Golda Meir:** The first woman prime minister of Israel.
- **John F. Kennedy:** The first Catholic president of the United States.

Important Dates

- **1945:** World War II ended.
- **1948:** The State of Israel was founded.
- **1967 and 1973:** Two of the wars between Israel and its Arab neighbors took place.

Terms Your Students Will Be Able to Define

- **British Mandate:** An order given by the League of Nations to Britain after the First World War to develop Palestine as a Jewish homeland.

Introducing the Lesson

You are a teenager in a displaced persons camp after the war. You have survived two years in a concentration camp, and now you can't find any of the members of your family. Your home was destroyed and you have no belongings. You are trying to get a visa to enter the United States, but there is a long wait and you are unable to get one.

Someone tells you that there is room for you on a ship that is sailing for Palestine. They are hoping that this place will become the new homeland for the Jews. You know that if you choose to go, you might be caught by the British and be sent to a detention camp in Cyprus. If you succeed in entering Palestine, you will be in a new place where you will know no one, a place that is threatened by war.

What should you do? Discuss the options.

Teaching Opportunities in the Text

Page 80 **But most of these 250,000 Jews were placed in special displaced persons (DP) camps set up by the Allied Forces.**
At the conclusion of the war, the actual fighting stopped, but it would be many years before those involved could recover from the destruction and loss that the war caused. What were some of the ways that European Jews continued to suffer after World War II ended?

Page 82 **Youth Aliyah**
The program of Youth Aliyah that began before World War II still exists today. Today Youth Aliyah supports Ethiopian and Russian immigrant children as well as Israeli children who come from troubled homes.

Page 83 **American Jews and the Jews of Israel**
List and discuss the many ways in which American Jews supported the land of Israel in the past and how this help is continued today.

Page 84 **The Jews of America joined the struggle for civil rights**
Why do you think there were so many Jews involved in fighting for the rights of black Americans? Which Jewish values does this concern reflect?

Page 85 **Shortly thereafter the years of black-Jewish unity came to an end....**
Today relations between African Americans and Jews are often strained. Why do you think this is so? What do you think caused this change to occur?

Page 86 **Looking Ahead**
What does the term "melting pot" mean? If America is a "melting pot," how would that situation affect Jewish culture and religion? Today we prefer to say that America is a "jigsaw puzzle or mosaic of cultures." Is that a healthier metaphor in terms of Jewish survival in America? Explain.

Jewish Value to Explore

▶ *Tzionut:* **Zionism.** Jewish people have always felt a special connection to the land of Israel. From the time of the destruction of the state by the Romans in 70 C.E., Jews have yearned to restore the state and create a Jewish homeland once again. This deep connection is founded both on religious and on political grounds.

Suggested Activities

1. Watch segments of the movie *Exodus* together, or suggest that the children watch it on their own.

2. You are a British citizen who objects to your country's policy of blockading Israeli ports to keep Jews from entering the country. Write a letter to the *London Times* expressing your views.

3. Design the front page of the newspaper the *Jerusalem Post* on May 14, 1948, the day that Israel declared its independence.

4. Research more about the life and work of Golda Meir. Present the information to the class. Perhaps your class would enjoy acting out selected scenes from her life such as the one described in the box "A Dangerous Mission" on page 83 of the textbook.

5. Pretend that there is a bill before Congress to provide Israel with $3 billion in foreign aid and loan guarantees. Assign one student to be a member of Congress who supports the State of Israel and the concept of foreign aid. Assign another student the role of one who supports the policy of isolationism. The rest of the class can be the other members of Congress. Have each

speaker present his or her point of view concerning U.S. foreign aid to Israel. Then Congress can vote on the bill. Perhaps you can add a few lobbyists in the mix.

6. A man named Dr. Louis Farakhan is going to come and speak at your school. While he is a very popular black leader, who tries to encourage blacks to improve themselves, he is also known as a man who made many anti-Semitic statements and been very hurtful to Jews. Some students in your school are very supportive of the visit, although some of them express discomfort with some of the things that Dr. Farakhan has said. As a Jewish student in the school, how do you react? Write a paragraph that describes your response to the situation.

Discussion Questions

1. What is a displaced persons camp? Who set them up? Why were they needed?

2. Discuss some of the ways American Jews tried to intervene to help the Jewish refugees of World War II.

3. Why were the British opposed to allowing Jews to settle in Palestine?

4. Smuggling people into places where they are not permitted to enter is an illegal activity. Why did the Jews engage in this widespread smuggling after World War II? Were their actions justified?

5. How was the State of Israel finally formed? What is its birthday?

6. What is Golda Meir best known for?

7. Why was it important to Jews that John Kennedy was elected president?

8. Why did Jews become so involved in the civil rights movement in America? Why has the relationship between Jews and African Americans changed so much in the last twenty years?

9. When Israel went to war with her Arab neighbors in 1967 and 1973, what were some of the things American Jews did to show support for Israel?

10. Why do we now call our country a "jigsaw puzzle or mosaic of cultures" rather than a "melting pot"?

Further Research Possibilities

Compile a list of the many ways in which American Jews offer support to Israel. Ask friends and family to fill out the survey and compile the results. If you discover any who have been involved in any special work for Israel or made a recent trip to Israel, invite them to speak to the class about their work or experience.

Primary Source Worksheet

Photocopy the black line master on the next page in the quantity you require and distribute a copy to each student. After your students have read the declaration, discuss the contents of the document.

1. What is Israel's immigration policy?

2. What rights are guaranteed to its citizens?

3. What message does it send to Arab neighbors?

4. What appeal does it make to Jews around the world?

Declaration of the Establishment of the State of Israel

▶ The Provisional Council of the State of Israel approved this declaration of May 14, 1948, and the State of Israel was born.

We, members of the people's council, representatives of the Jewish community of Eretz-Israel and of the Zionist movement, are here assembled on the day of the termination of the British mandate over Eretz-Israel and, by virtue of our resolution of the United Nations General Assembly, hereby declare the establishment of a Jewish state in Eretz-Israel, to be known as the state of Israel.

THE STATE OF ISRAEL will be open for Jewish immigration and for the Ingathering of the exiles; it will foster the development of the country for the benefit of all its habitants; it will based on freedom, justice and peace as envisaged by the prophets of Israel; it will ensure complete equality of social and political rights to all its inhabitants irrespective of religion, race or sex; it will guarantee freedom of religion, conscience, language, education and culture; it will safeguard the Holy Places of all religions; and it will be faithful to the principles of the Charter of the United Nations.

WE EXTEND our hand to all neighbouring states and their peoples in an offer of peace and good neighbourliness, and appeal to them to establish bonds of cooperation and mutual help with the sovereign Jewish people settled in its own land. The State of Israel is prepared to do its share in common effort for the advancement of the entire Middle East.

WE APPEAL to the Jewish people throughout the diaspora to rally around the Jews of Eretz-Israel in the tasks of immigration and upbuilding and to stand by them in the great struggle for the realization of the age-old dream—the redemption of Israel.

Placing our trust in the almighty, we affix our signatures to this proclamation at this session of the Provisional Council of State, on the soil of the homeland, in the city of Tel-Aviv on this Sabbath eve, the 5th day of Iyar, 5708 (14th May, 1948).

12 Jewish Life in America Today

Let Freedom Ring (pages 87-93)

Chapter Overview

Even though Jews have always been a small minority in the United States, we are responsible for a large number of contributions to American society. Over the years we have successfully incorporated Jewish values into the American way of life.

Challenges as well as opportunities face us in the future. We are looking at a future in which we will need to care for a large aging population and an increasingly large population of Jews living in poverty. Divorce is becoming more and more common in the Jewish community too. We will need to deal with issues of identity, clarify the role of women in religious practice, and explore our feelings concerning homosexual men and women.

We will need to help thousands of new immigrants adjust to life in Israel and America and will have to support the State of Israel as she seeks peace with her Arab neighbors.

The challenges and opportunities of the future belong to us. How shall we make the most of them?

Important Events Your Students Will Witness

- **Operation Exodus:** When thousands of Russian immigrants were brought to Israel and the United States to begin new lives of religious freedom.

Places Your Students Will Visit

- **Washington, D.C., in 1987:** Where nearly one-quarter of a million Jews from all over the United States demonstrated on behalf of Jews trapped in the Soviet Union.

People Your Students Will Meet Along the Way

- **Prime Minister Rabin, King Hussein and President Clinton:** The three parties who worked out the peace treaty between Jordan and Israel.

Introducing the Lesson

1. Each chapter of this book has described the work of Jewish men and women who have struggled to incorporate Jewish values into American life. Ask your students to recall some of these people and the values they lived by. Create a chart that depicts the many ways we have brought Jewish values to American life.

73

OR

2. Ask the students to brainstorm a list of the five most important challenges that face American Jews in the future. Discuss some of the actions we might take to meet each one of those challenges. Post your list in chart form and compare your choice with those in the text when you have finished studying the chapter.

Teaching Opportunities in the Text

Page 87 **But, as you will see, these are not only challenges but also opportunities—opportunities for us to build a better future as Americans and Jews.** What is meant by a challenge? How can a challenge be turned into an opportunity? Give an example of a challenge that can be successfully met by turning it into an opportunity.

Pages 88-89 **The Jewish Population in the United States (1993)**
What are some of the challenges of being a minority? What are some of the personal ways this status affects us in our everyday lives? Are there positive aspects to being a minority?

Page 89 **The Aged in the Jewish Community**
Many aged people require special attention because they are ill or too feeble to leave their homes. Many have lost family and friends and suffer from loneliness. What are some mitzvot that we are called upon to perform for the elderly in our communities? How can we accomplish these goals?

Page 91 **Who Is a Jew?**
The question of "Who is a Jew?" was always a simple one with a simple, legal answer. Traditionally, a Jew is a person whose mother is Jewish. America has complicated this issue, however, by offering people the freedom to make choices of their own. Jews do not live under one halachic authority any more. Is the new-found freedom a healthy thing for Judaism in America or is it something that will cause the weakening of our religion?

Page 93 **The State of Israel**
Many changes are taking place on the world scene today. Ask your students to list some of these (Large population shifts as Jews emigrate from Russia, Ethiopia, and Arab nations to the United States and Israel; the evolution of the peace process in Israel; changing borders in Israel; the rapid rate of Jewish assimilation in the United States, etc.). How will these changes affect us as Americans and as Jews? How will they affect our future?

Jewish Value to Explore

Most of the challenges presented in this chapter are accompanied by a textual quote that suggests the Jewish value we will need to call upon in dealing with that particular issue. Discuss each quote as it comes up in the text. Add others as they come to mind. Discuss how Jewish values direct our actions.

▶ *Tikkun Olam*, **Repairing the World.** The text ends by extending a personal challenge to each student to become active in shaping the Jewish future in America. They are challenged to use their talents in a positive way to improve the lives of others and to build a safe and secure Jewish future. Each Jew is commanded to take personal responsibility for shaping a better world.

Suggested Activities

1. Take the list of challenges you made for "Introducing the Lesson" and compare it with the selections of the author of the text. Discuss each one, along with the paths we must take in dealing with the problem. Perhaps you would like to assign each student one challenge to explore. Have each child report their thoughts on each issue to the class.

2. Use Jewish values to direct problem solving. List some of the issues facing American Jews today. List the specific values we should use in dealing with each issue. Create specific solutions based on Jewish values.

3. Trace the progress of women's issues throughout this book. Who were some of the important women who shaped the struggle for equal rights for women? What were some of the major events that affected the status of women in America? Equal liturgical rights for women in synagogue are a natural outgrowth of this movement. Write a paragraph explaining how you feel about the changes that have occurred in regard to women's participation in religious life.

4. Interview a new Russian immigrant in your community. Ask about his or her experience in coming to America and the experiences in adjusting to a new way of life. Perhaps the person might find time to speak to the class about these experiences.

5. Ask students to consider their futures as American Jews. Ask each student to write a concluding essay expressing his or her feelings about the future. What do they see as the most difficult challenges? What do they wish to accomplish, both personally as Jews and for the community as a whole? Bind these into a book and make a copy for each student.

Discussion Questions

1. List and discuss the many ways Jews have brought Torah values to American life.

2. Why do you think Jews have made so many important contributions to American life despite our minority status?

3. What are some of the challenges American Jews face in the future?

4. Use the chart on page 88 to name the five states that have the largest percentage of Jewish population.

5. How has freedom created new issues for the American Jewish community?

6. How will the recent large immigration from Russia to Israel and America create change for the Jewish community?

7. What is our personal role in meeting the challenges of the future for the American Jewish community?

8. What would be lost if America's Jewish community were to disappear?

Further Research Possibilities

What is the Jewish population of your city or town? What percentage of the overall population is that? Has this statistic changed over the last several years? If so, how and why? How do these statistics affect your life as a Jew in your community?

Use the statistics and photographs to create a bulletin board display of Jewish life in your city or town.

N • O • T • E • S